Praise for *Hel*

"*Hello? Who Is This? Margaret?* is a find. It's a series of sometimes rollicking and sometimes tragedy-bounding but always amusing essays of a girl who starts on a path to a life in show business but gets diverted. From the West Coast to the East Coast to Prague, the essays take us on a journey best described as a report from a woman living as a modern-day member of the Lost Generation. To grasp the breadth, depth, and fascination of the life being depicted, you have to read the book."

—**Mark Lonow,** co-owner of the World
Famous Improv and actor

"Dani Alpert has the uncanny ability to make you laugh while also being brutally honest, especially about herself. Her essays are so richly detailed that you feel like you're a passenger on her poignantly funny adventures, from a bleak hotel in a desolate part of Prague, to her parents' house in the suburbs, to her encounters with celebrities. Even when things don't go the way she hoped they would, Alpert manages to find the encouragement and inspiration to keep going. And we find ourselves cheering for her success while laughing at the many obstacles in her way."

—**Scott Blakeman,** comedian

"*Hello? Who Is This? Margaret?* is a front-row seat to the inner workings of a woman with a wildly imaginative comic mind. Get swept up in these laugh-out-loud personal stories and Dani's refusal to let heartbreak or having a few dreams dashed ever get the best of her."

—**Dani Klein Modisett,** founder and
CEO of Laughter On Call and author
of *Take My Spouse, Please*

"Readers will laugh, but often with small tears of pity and recognition, as Alpert's humor dares to reveal relatable sorrow, frustration, and awkwardness. Every stumble recounted here, though, becomes a learning experience, and Alpert moves forward with a persistence that could put even the most spoiled or stubborn child to shame. What's equally impressive is her self-awareness. Readers witness her ability to reflect, to grow, and to truly see herself. She understands that our limitations are self-imposed and that no one else gets to decide where we stop or what we're capable of becoming.

Better still, Alpert knows when to pause, reflect, and give weight to the moments that matter, all without sacrificing the laughs. Her writing feels alive, deeply personal, like she is discovering the meaning of these experiences alongside her readers, who will cheer her in seizing victories whenever and however they come."

—*PW* BookLife

"*Hello? Who Is This? Margaret?* is a funny and heartfelt essay collection that models leaping into the unknown and growing into oneself in the process. . . . [It] muses through life events with sarcasm and hope."

—*Foreword* Clarion Reviews

"Alpert writes with humor, honesty, and hope. Regardless of what is thrown her way, she perseveres, finding new ways to plow through difficulties and chase after her dreams—even those that need to be dusted off and rearranged."

—Chanticleer Book Reviews

"Even when we were kids at theater camp, Dani showed confidence, humor, and moxie. I know readers will enjoy *Hello? Who Is This? Margaret?* as much as I did. Like Dani, this book has it all."

—Allan Murray, stand-up comedian

Kelly—

Hello?
Who Is This?
Margaret?

essays

Dani Alpert

Thanks for reading!

RIVER GROVE
BOOKS

Dani

The names and identifying characteristics of some persons referenced in this book, as well as identifying events and places, have been changed to protect the privacy of the individuals and their families.

Published by River Grove Books
Austin, TX
www.rivergrovebooks.com

Distributed by River Grove Books

Design and composition by Greenleaf Book Group
Cover design by Greenleaf Book Group
Cover image used under license from Adobe Stock: 374915240/Carpio Photography

Versions of some chapters were previously published in other works:

Dani Alpert, "Between Fantasy and Reality Is a Stripper Pole," *The ManifestStation*, January 2, 2025, https://www.themanifeststation.net/2025/01/02/fantasy-stripper-pole.

Dani Alpert, "Bathrooms Without Borders," in *The Girlfriend Mom: A Memoir* (Little Ricky Press, 2020).

Dani Alpert, "I Came out of an Orthodox Jewish California Closet," *Jewish Literary Journal*, May 2024, https://jewishliteraryjournal.com/creative-non-fiction/i-came-out-of-an-orthodox-jewish-california-closet-dani-alpert.

Publisher's Cataloging-in-Publication data is available.

Print ISBN: 978-1-966629-19-1

eBook ISBN: 978-1-966629-20-7

First Edition

Contents

A Note from the Author

I'VE CHANGED THE NAMES OF some individuals, except in the case of my family. They is what they is. If those portrayed beg to differ with my recollections, to that I say, write your own book and tell your own story. Several timelines have been compressed for dramatic effect. In some cases, I've exaggerated the truth to make a point or get a bigger laugh. The stories were written as I remembered them. In the essay "Celebrity Adjacent," I refer to Chaz Bono as Chas, the name he went by during the year covered in that essay. The book is not a courtroom transcript, but it is emotionally sound.

The ▆▆▆▆▆ Agency

November 17, 1994

Danielle,

Enclosed is your pay check for week ending October 28. I have deducted Friday, October 21, and Friday, October 28 (as additional days off that you took) as well as all your long distance calls. Such calls came to $106.77.

▆▆▆▆▆▆▆▆▆▆▆▆▆▆▆▆▆▆▆▆▆▆▆▆▆▆ A bit of advice: Hollywood is a small town and people's word and honor defines their credibility. Be careful who you fuck.

one

Czech-ing Out of Prague

THE STORY IS AS OLD as dirt. The kid doesn't get enough attention from her parents, so she seeks external approval on a stage in front of an audience of strangers. My parents didn't applaud or cheer when I entered a room or did headstands on the kitchen counter. Tough crowd, those two. What did they think was going to happen?

The moment I knew I wanted to perform was during my first song and dance recital when I was seven. The combination of feeling people staring at me and wearing a sparkly costume was thrilling. My fellow hoofers and I wore pink ballet slippers and leotards with white fringe—like flappers wore in the 1920s, which was spot-on because we sang that Tin Pan Alley chart topper "Baby Face" from 1926. I loved the leotard so much that it was my Halloween costume for the next two years, even though I'd clearly outgrown it. I told people I was a Vegas showgirl. However, my mom insisted that I wear a coat when we went trick-or-treating.

There we were, a glittering gaggle of peewee entertainers, standing shoulder to shoulder, swaying to the music with both hands pressed against our hearts, singing, "I didn't need a shove, 'cause I just fell in love with your pretty baby face." We belted out the last note, and the dance studio owner and choreographer, Miss Pike, motioned to us from offstage in the wings to take a bow. The applause hit me like a thunderclap. I thought the clapping was just for me—like the audience had recognized my exceptional aptitude for standing on my toes or waving. But I'm sure everyone thought the applause was just for them.

The notion that I could command the attention of strangers by doing something that was fun and came naturally to me was powerful and intoxicating.

Nothing was ever the same after that.

Much of my childhood was spent watching television variety shows, like *Donny & Marie* and *The Carol Burnett Show*. Those shows and the reruns of *I Love Lucy* were my earliest inspirations. Lucy got me thinking that character work was just as important as singing and dancing and that I should also sharpen those skills if I was going to be a star. I made up childish accents that were unintelligible and had deep gibberish-y conversations with my stuffed animals. My mom gave me some of her old makeup, and I'd cake it on really thick. Then, using a lip pencil (it could've been an eyeliner, I didn't know), I outlined my lips like a visually impaired clown. I'd drag a line from the corner of my mouth to my hairline—perhaps my character was in a horrible car accident and had been disfigured. I'd contort my face and practice my transformations in front of the bathroom mirror for hours. And it was exciting to see how ugly or unrecognizable I could make myself. I don't like to use the word "genius," but I could look downright grotesque.

Too bad Vaudeville was dead—now that really spoke to me.

Years of dance classes, acting schools, voice lessons, and a subscription to *Backstage* followed. I kept a running list of the directors I wanted to work with in the future and talent agents I wanted to represent me—all names I'd found in the New York Yellow Pages. For you youngins, the Yellow (and White) Pages were essentially a hard copy of the internet and are now essentially irrelevant.

My goals were pretty superficial at first. I fantasized about autograph seekers finding me at recess in grade school, disturbing me in checkout lines while shopping with my mom, and intruding on family dinners at restaurants. It's a bit embarrassing to admit, but sometimes I'd pretend that a limousine was following me, like when I'd walk to a friend's house or tennis practice. I imagined the car stopping, the back window lowering, and a movie producer handing me his card and asking me to call him. He'd been looking for someone like me for an upcoming project. I was discovered! I never decided what it was about me that made him pull over, but the details were beside the point.

International fame was the only acceptable outcome—magazine covers, scandalous gossip, having a stalker level of international fame. And I did everything possible to see that it happened.

For the most part, my parents were very supportive. They came to every performance and encouraged me to spend three consecutive summers at theater camp. Although, I think that was more for them, so they'd have two months alone. But when I was twelve and I told them about my true aspirations—a career in entertainment and global stardom—they didn't take me seriously. No one in my family ever discussed a career in the performing arts—it was either the cliché doctor, lawyer, or teacher. Still, I thought they would've been more understanding. My mother is a talented fine artist; my father can hold his own with any comedian, past or present. But that day in the family room, they had the audacity to call my passion "a hobby"— something I'd probably (hopefully?) grow out of. I lost my shit on them and paced around, emoting for fifteen minutes.

"What do you think I've been doing all these years?" I wailed, pulling at my ponytail. "This is not a dress rehearsal. This is my life."

It's also highly possible that they felt this way because I could be exhausting.

"It's a simple question," my mom might say. "Baked potato or fries?"

"You know starch makes me bloat. It's opening night!" I'd answer, beating my chest, all drama queeny. "Why are you trying to sabotage me?"

So my parents supported me in a way that was comfortable for them—from the sidelines while writing a check. In hindsight, perhaps they were just acting like concerned parents who wanted the best chance of happiness and success for their child. They'd seen how dejected and demoralized I'd been after my fifth-grade chorus audition.

The chorus class gathered on risers in the lunchroom, which doubled as an auditorium. The music teacher, Mrs. Hillard, a squat woman with pockmarked cheeks, sat at the piano and accompanied each student as they stepped up and sang scales.

Not for one minute did I think I wouldn't make the chorus. Why would I? I'd been singing in my room for years, despite everyone telling me I might be tone-deaf. What did my family know?

They weren't professionals. I practiced singing along to my favorite show tunes behind closed doors. "If you're blue, and you don't know where to go to . . ." Without fail, my brother would pound on the shared wall between our bedrooms, pleading, "Stop! Why don't *you* go where I don't have to listen to this shit. You are so weird."

When it was my turn, I stood proud and joined Mrs. Hillard at the piano.

I sang, "Do, re, mi, fa, so, la, ti, do." Unfortunately, my "fa" went off the rails, and I couldn't recover. The last "do" was sharp *and* flat. I sounded like a cat in heat being dragged into traffic by its tail.

This first significant defeat went down in my big book of rejections and disappointments.

My parents absorbed my pain as their own, and that's why they tried to dissuade me from a life of suffering—because they didn't want to suffer. They'd toss out statistics, hoping that I'd be scared straight. "You know, only 2 percent of aspiring performers actually 'make it.'" They thought they could protect me from the soul-crushing reality of show business. That was sweet of them—and also a waste of time. My desires and dreams were too fierce and bullish. Reality, parental concerns, and shitty odds never stood a chance.

By the time I got to high school, my ego had swelled to a sizable proportion despite the few achievements I'd collected up to that point. It didn't matter, though, because my magical thinking had convinced me otherwise. In my mind, my inflated ego tracked and seemed justified. At sixteen, I convinced myself that no one in my theater group was as talented as I was. And I often bragged about how much I knew about Broadway. This was mainly based on the fact that I could sing the entire soundtrack to several Broadway musicals. At the very least, sharing the information made me feel like I was somehow part of the Broadway community. And at the most, it let me believe that I was practically "on" Broadway. I hoped that my fellow thespians saw it the same way.

At that age, how could I know that my superior attitude was a defense against my deep insecurities—my looks (think Chelsea Clinton, the White House years) and my abilities (could I actually be tone-deaf?). It was the only way to mask how I honestly felt about myself. The theater—frankly, all of the performing arts—was the safest hiding place I knew.

One day, I approached Mr. Sherman, the acting teacher, who also directed most of our school plays. I'd already worked with professional theater directors and thought he was inexperienced. He thought I was showy and bossy. He wasn't wrong.

"What about doing the musical *Runaways*, by Elizabeth Swados, this year? I was recently in it." I was being generous. It was an Off-Off-Off Broadway production at the Carter Theater, inside the old Carter Hotel in Times Square. Shortly after the curtain came down, the city razed the building for health violations (it was named one of America's dirtiest hotels), and it had been a hub for homicides. The show had just one Tuesday matinee performance, but Mr. Sherman didn't need to know that.

Mr. Sherman lifted his bifocals and rested them on top of his bald head. "I'm not familiar with the show."

"It's about kids who run away from broken homes or orphanages and live on the streets. They share their horrible childhoods through song, dance, and spoken word."

Mr. Sherman grabbed a hand-sized bust of Shakespeare from his desk and stared at it. "Seems risky."

The town I grew up in was preppy, affluent, and suburban.

I could see how my classmates and their parents might have had trouble relating to the subject matter. What did they know about life on the streets, drug dealers, and prostitution? I argued, "Aren't we all running away from something?" I said that if the song and dance numbers had high production values, then no one would be paying attention to the simulated smoking and sexual innuendos. Also, I was now an expert on the show and could help Mr. Sherman if he needed me to step in. I thought about the praise my peers and the townsfolk would heap on me for being a visionary and bringing a cutting-edge and raw piece of theater to our high school.

"Let's shake things up, Mr. Sherman," I said. "How many times can we do *Our Town?*"

Mr. Sherman relented, and except for a few parents who complained about the political undertones and graphic tales of child abuse, *Runaways* was a huge success.

I was just getting started.

After college, I moved to Los Angeles (more on college later; patience), where I continued following my North Star. Professionally speaking, I believed I had a better chance of making it in LA because there were more opportunities than in New York. The theater was my first love, but television and film were the Holy Grail. When I arrived, I could hardly believe it. After all of my planning, pursuing, and commitment to my art and global stardom, it was all falling into place. My hard work and talent would be acknowledged—at last.

I zigzagged from job to job, staying in perpetual motion, which was easy to do in my twenties. The jobs weren't always in my field of interest because I didn't always have a choice—I had to eat. Still, with every job, including but not limited to gofer, prop assistant, location scout, and animal wrangler, I stayed hopeful.

Unfortunately, as the years passed, my attempts were only slightly rewarded—just enough yeses to keep me hanging on— circling the drain one day and booking a part in a low-budget, nonspeaking role in a corporate training video the next. Most of my friends were in the same boat. And often we were each other's life vests. We celebrated each other's wins and comforted each other over the losses. We were young, energized, and determined— aspiring artists paying our dues.

I even tried modeling.

SFX: Sad trombone.

I cut my long hair in my early thirties and went super short. Several people told me the gamine look was in and convinced me that with my new cut, I'd most certainly get work "in television commercials or print." That's all I needed to hear, and I updated my headshot. I was always updating my headshot. It could be the key to unlocking a life-changing audition. New haircut? New headshot. New hair color? New headshot. Weight gain? Headshot. Heat rash? Headshot.

When I saw the new round of photos, I thought, "Wow, I am a model." The next day, I walked into a prestigious agency on Melrose Avenue unannounced and asked to speak to their commercial agent. And then I was politely ushered out. Wow, I had some elephant-sized balls back then. Ah, the power of delusion. I had to believe my new haircut was my ticket to that life-changing audition—I was running out of options. But, come on, Alpert, a model?

By the time I was in my late thirties, people I'd started the journey with had made names for themselves and a few were now in the 2 percent. Others had left the business and moved to farms in Vermont or started families in Scotland in favor of more predictable lives. But I held steadfast. I fell into writing for reality TV shows and then wrote screenplays. I did stand-up comedy for a while and even taught comedy traffic school. Hold your applause.

Did I mention that I didn't know or care where or in what form my big break would come?

I wore my stick-to-itiveness (read: stubbornness) like a badge of honor. Never giving up hope, I was sure that what I wanted was waiting for me right around the next corner—in the next lunch meeting, the next freelance gig, next, next, next.

But what I was really thinking was, *Who do I have to blow?* Clearly, I hadn't slept with the right people—not that anyone had asked.

My parents' early fears came true. My self-esteem had shrunk to the size of a mushroom cap. At thirty-eight, it was getting harder to hear "almost," "so close," or "not quite" over and over from the industry that I loved. I wondered if I should've zigged when I zagged.

One day, a friend told me about a talent agent she knew who was looking for an assistant. It wasn't my first or seventh choice, but I needed the work. I interviewed and was hired on the spot. I spent my days emailing scripts to B-list actors and alphabetizing their demo reels. A blindfolded paraplegic chimpanzee could have done the job. The only upsides to working in an office were the office supplies I occasionally swiped and the long-distance calls I occasionally made. The agent I assisted, Beverly Lawson, started each day announcing when she was heading to the crapper, with an issue of *Variety* tucked neatly under her arm. Ew.

The universe was definitely trying to tell me something.

On one painfully slow afternoon, I overheard Shelley, the receptionist, and Kevin, our mailroom intern, laughing loudly. I went out to investigate.

"Shelley taught English in Peru," Kevin squealed.

"Really?" I asked, intrigued.

"Yeah," Shelley said while flipping through the office issue of *Variety*. (Double ew.) "I got certified in a school in Prague, and then I went on the road. Wild, right?"

Wild, indeed. A surge of energy shot up my spine. Maybe it was time to stop digging, and throw in the towel.

"Myanmar was the best," Shelley continued.

Could I actually give up? Turn my back on the only life I knew? Try something different? What if holding on all these years was holding me back?

Walking away from Hollywood wasn't a new thought. But usually, when it popped up, I'd immediately think, *And do what?* How could I quit? I'd been telling everyone "I'm going to be a star!" since I was seven. I imagined my high school theater group and my Aunt Tillie remarking, "I guess she couldn't cut it."

My pride was holding me back.

It was impossible to think I couldn't cut it despite knowing that "making it" and having a successful career wasn't just about talent, hard work, and perseverance. I'd hear quotes like, "Better to have tried and failed than to have never tried at all," by the author Sean-Paul Thomas. Or Thomas Edison's, "I have not failed. I've just found ten thousand ways that won't work." And I'd think, *Sean-Paul and Thomas can kiss my ass.* I took the quotes to mean that all of my work had been in vain. I didn't (yet) have the maturity or perspective to see this wasn't true.

But the assistant job made me feel like I was back where I'd started—repeating work I'd already done. I was moving in reverse and praying that I could somehow run over myself. I could barely remember my original dream and what I'd hoped to accomplish by moving out to LA. Did I still have the desire? I used to take comfort in believing that the struggles and endless parade of noes were building up to the big payoff. But listening to Shelley that day, I threw a flag on the play. *This is bullshit. What the fuck was I doing alphabetizing actors' demo tapes?!*

I drilled Shelley with questions for half an hour while she fumbled with the multiline desk phone and repeatedly hung up on callers. I pulled up the world map in my mind, painting a picture of all the places teaching would take me. The following day, I quit.

I enrolled in the four-week certification program. I was going off-script, but if showbiz wasn't going to give me any love, I'd look for it in the Czech Republic.

Choke on that, Hollywood.

Maybe teaching in Prague was my calling. And then, if I was lucky, Bahrain or South Korea. It was a bold move—anyone would agree.

I threw my Rolodex (this was 2005) and the stacks of headshots and resumes into a box and taped it shut. Everything else I owned, from spatula to car, I sold in a two-day yard sale before I left Los Angeles. Whatever I couldn't sell, I donated—I didn't want anything dragging me down, not even a spatula. Random people from Craigslist came to my apartment, and I didn't even check their IDs. Nor did I ask them to take off their shoes—very unlike me. Instead, I watched in a Zen state as they hauled off my microwave and portable dishwasher. "I hope it brings you as much joy as it brought me," I said to two face-tattooed men carrying my shabby chic sofa over their heads and disappearing into the night.

After three flights on three different airlines, including a precious-sounding EasyJet, and two rain delays, I arrived at Ruzyne International Airport. My suitcase, crammed with the sparse remains of my material life, did not. I wondered if I'd ever see my *All That Jazz* and *Arrested Development* DVDs again.

The school I was attending had arranged for someone to collect me at the airport, but I worried my delays would leave me stranded. I'd accidentally left my cell phone in the bathroom at LAX and I had no way of contacting the school. I considered exchanging money and finding a pay phone. And I might have actually done it had I not been suddenly overpowered by anxiety and inertia. *Where do I go? How do I get there?*

Suddenly, finding a currency exchange kiosk and a pay phone were skills reserved for licensed professionals. *What the hell?!* I stood frozen in the middle of the airport, helpless and lost. I'd forgotten how to travel and be a person outside of my Hollywood bubble.

Over the years, I suppose my goals had hamstrung me in Los Angeles. I didn't travel other than back East for a holiday here and there or a bris. I didn't do much of anything that wasn't in service of my goal. What if I was away and missed *the* call? And now, in the airport, I was like a hatchling, peering out into a new world, waddling in circles in search of food and the customer service desk to see about my lost suitcase.

Once the paperwork was filed to report it lost, I went outside. I stood under the taxi and hotel shuttle banners alongside visor-wearing tourists. Any minute, my town car would pull up with a driver wearing a chauffeur cap holding a sign with my name on it. The more time that passed, however, the more self-conscious I got. Despite appearing completely disoriented in the airport, I also didn't want to be confused for a tourist. I had a local mailing address. A visa. I was practically a Praguer. I wasn't visiting for a few days of sightseeing and cheap beer—I'd expatriated! I was special!

After twenty minutes of waiting for my ride in the hot summer sun (my sunscreen and hat were in my lost suitcase, and I was getting melanoma for sure), a nondescript white passenger van pulled up in front of me. A gruff-looking man in his sixties stepped down and bounded toward me, shouting something in Czech. He unceremoniously introduced himself, and I handed him my identification. He grabbed my carry-on luggage, tossed it into the van's cargo area, and opened the front passenger door. *Odd*, I thought. There were plenty of empty seats in the back. Who was he saving them for? It was just the two of us. Why did I have to sit in the front? It was an intimate proposition—I hardly knew the man.

A heartbeat later, the seating mystery was solved. A group of statuesque silver-haired adults came running toward the van. Mr. Gruff checked their IDs, slid the side door open, and they piled in. *They aren't also going to my school, are they?* Then Mr. Gruff opened the front passenger door again and shooed me into the middle seat. One of the women slid in next to me, and we uncomfortably acknowledged one another.

"They're from Norway," Mr. Gruff said as he climbed up behind the steering wheel. *Oh, so you do speak English.* I pulled the seat belt strap across my chest in silence, offended over having to relinquish my window seat for a stick shift up my ass. Apparently, Nordic DNA trumps Lithuanian American Jew. Hmm.

The Norwegians laughed and screamed joyfully behind me as we made our way out of the airport. I turned to my seatmate. "Is this your first time in Prague?"

She nodded.

"Me too," I answered. I waited for her to reciprocate, because that's how conversations work. And when she didn't, I persisted, hoping to make a connection—that's how I work.

"I have a Norwegian writer friend in Los Angeles," I continued. She ignored me and focused her attention on the scenery whipping by. I didn't take it personally. She probably wished she was yukking it up in the back with her friends. It made me think of my friends back home.

The decision to pull up my LA roots had been undeniable and uncomplicated. I hadn't considered the impact of leaving my friends and giving up everything I knew or ever wanted. Not once did I think that Dani's big adventure wouldn't work out. I was that confident. This next chapter of my life and all its possibilities was bigger than the doubts now swirling around my head. I'd traded in my Hollywood fantasies for living in Bogotá and Vang Vieng. I'd climb Kilimanjaro on my day off, not to mention the bragging rights that come with a passport full of colorful stamps. I'd cut the cord, giving myself permission to stop struggling. I felt twenty pounds lighter—give or take.

But before I hired a sherpa to take me up Kilimanjaro, I had to get through this uncomfortable van ride with the band of Vikings.

Gruff pulled up to the front of an upscale and modern hotel in Wenceslas Square, and the Vikings disembarked. Considering that Prague had almost sixteen years to reform and spruce up the place since the Velvet Revolution, I assumed the school would also be modernized and remodeled.

But as Gruff and I drove farther away from the city, the neighborhoods got bleaker. Rows of gray prefabricated concrete apartment buildings populated block after block. *Oh, dear.* We pulled into a dirt parking lot of a two-story brick-and-glass building. It reminded me of the library in the town where I grew up—indistinct and uninteresting. Gruff dropped my carry-on on the ground, and I grabbed it before it tipped into a mud puddle. He climbed back into the van and drove off without a goodbye or a tip. I was left to drag my luggage over dirt and rocks into the building on my own.

As I entered, a smiley young woman with braces greeted me from her seat behind a plastic card table in the hallway.

"Hello. Welcome to TEFL Worldwide Prague," she said, handing me an orange folder. "This has everything you'll need while you're in school: calendars, schedules, and the dos and don'ts of life in Prague." She was exceptionally upbeat and efficient. "I called you a cab to take you to your hotel. Unfortunately, our school driver had to leave because your flight was delayed."

"Really?" I asked. She nodded. I'd made this brave move, relocating to Prague to start a new life, and she was calling me a cab? I seethed quietly. I wanted to tell her that this was a big deal. That I was a big deal! I wasn't necessarily expecting the red-carpet treatment, but some acknowledgment would've been nice. I didn't have to fly six thousand miles to feel unexceptional. I could've stayed in LA.

I'd opted for off-campus housing at a hotel because, once I turned twenty-five, I stopped sharing bedrooms and bathrooms with people—including family and most friends. As a freshman in college, I lived with two roommates, which was inhumane. It was

forced intimacy. Making three eighteen-year-olds, all with different dietary needs and tastes in music and television, cohabit in a
small room for nine months should be considered a war crime.
I'd hung a thin cotton tapestry around my bed like a canopy, for
some privacy—or at least the illusion of privacy. Needless to say,
it failed to block out the sounds of my roommates screwing their
boyfriends a foot away from my head. The uncivility even happened on school nights.

Back to Prague.

A cab pulled up to the front of the school. I climbed in the back
with my small suitcase. The driver glanced in the rearview mirror,
raised his eyebrows, and shook his head. It was the same look my
brother gave me when my mom made him drive me to softball
practice because she was running late for her pottery class. I worried
he wouldn't accept American dollars or a credit card. How serious
could I have been about Prague if I didn't know what currency was
accepted? And the extent of my Czech was *ahoj* (hello). I'd only
listened to one chapter of the Pimsleur language-learning CDs a
friend had gotten me because it was boring.

In my defense, the school's brochure said that knowing Czech
wasn't a prerequisite. Even so, I typically do more research when
I'm invited to a party than I did before moving to Prague. I want
to know if there will be food, or if I should eat beforehand. If the
party is at a restaurant, is there wait service or is it a buffet? I hate
buffets—they're petri dishes of hair strands and dead skin cells. Is
the host paying? Is it cash only? I may even ask the host who I'll be
sitting next to and prepare topics of conversation.

I leaned forward in the cab, waved a dollar bill next to the
driver's head as if he were a male stripper, and nodded *yes?* while

I screamed, "Is this okay?" I was everything I hated about Americans traveling abroad. The driver turned and shook his head *no*. I decided against shoving my American Express card in his face.

"Can we stop at a bank so I can exchange money?" Surely he'd recognize the word bank. He grunted and peeled out of the school parking lot.

As I stared out the window, the landscape grew darker and danker. Finally, we pulled up to the Czech National Bank. My driver hmphed as I got out.

"Dude," I wanted to say, "the curtain came down. What's with the moral outrage? You've got a job, which is more than I can say."

———

I stared up at the Hotel Pramen from the back seat. *What have I done?*

It was a towering stucco-and-concrete building—circa whenever Stalinist architecture was all the rage. Random windows were missing on each of the twelve floors. The building was weathered and worn, colored in faded reds and blues. The parking lot was empty except for piles of bricks and deflated tires and dreams. You know that moment when that shiny new thing you'd been excitedly planning for and imagining becomes a reality? And then you shudder and moan, "Man, was I wrong. This isn't anything like I thought it would be." That.

I attempted to dull these early signs of regret and not judge a book by its Socialist Classicism building cover. *The interior will definitely be updated and stylish. My room will have a window, and the shower will have good water pressure. I'll slip into a light cotton waffle-weave robe—perfect for summer—that's hanging on the back of the bathroom door. I'll curl up on the comfy bed and moisturize my tired and callused heels.*

It had to be a hundred degrees in the lobby. The only pieces of furniture were two black leather couches hemorrhaging white stuffing. A man in white leggings with exposed hirsute shoulders played sinister carnival music on an electric keyboard in the corner. I checked in with the stern-looking woman behind the front desk wearing a *schmatta* on her head. In broken English, she told me that breakfast wasn't included in my thirteen-dollar-per-night rate. Breakfast was the least of my worries.

The wheels of my carry-on luggage echoed on the tiled floors as I rolled it down the hallway to my assigned room. It was every abandoned state hospital in a psychodrama movie. I expected to see a female warden in a form-fitting uniform with giant cartoon keys dangling from her waistband jump out of the shadows. "You better get some sleep," she threatens. "Tomorrow's a big day."

I unlocked the door to my room and gasped. It was the size of a shoebox—and where I would live for a month. It smelled of goulash and mothballs. There was no air-conditioning, and two lonely wire hangers hung in the dark pine wardrobe. I was one of the lucky ones with a window—although it only opened a claustrophobic six inches. I could barely squeeze my head through the crack. A garbage dumpster was positioned directly below, and beyond the chain-link fence was a forest that looked like a perfect place to hide a body.

My lazy approach to researching Prague also meant I hadn't asked questions like, "Can you describe the housing?" before I signed up. Had I seen photos of the hotel before mailing my deposit, it may have given me pause. Although, I doubted anything, including accommodations better suited for a convict, could've stopped me. I was afraid that if I'd done a deep dive and truly thought about what I was doing, I might've bailed. Shelley told me that the school guaranteed a teaching job after graduation, and I'd see the world. What more did I need to know?

I placed my backpack on the floor and sat on the twin bed. *Ouch.* The mattress was as thick as a ream of paper and just as firm. There wasn't a full-length mirror, but the elevator had one, so there was that. An old portable radio sat on a shelf above the desk. After I fiddled with the knob and walked around the room a bit, I got reception for one English-speaking music station. However, after hearing James Blunt's "You're Beautiful" five times in one hour, I welcomed the local Czech rock 'n' roll. There was one electrical outlet. Several petrified towels were piled on the bed beside some extra rolls of toilet paper—toilet paper that could sand unfinished wood.

I dropped my head in my hands. Tears welled.

Why did I sell everything and make it so permanent? Maybe I just needed a vacation.

Breathe. Take a shower and change your underwear. You'll feel better after a good night's sleep.

Unfortunately, clean underwear and every other article of clothing I owned were in my missing suitcase. So I slept in my two-day-old clothes. I also didn't trust the sheets to be fresh, so I slept on top of them. And I wanted to be ready when the warden came to collect me at dawn.

My suitcase arrived early the following morning, and I gratefully changed into clean clothes. I had one day to wander the city before school orientation. And, like a local Praguer, I ran errands. Maybe I'd take in a cathedral or a bridge—I assumed the city had them. I made a mental note to pick up a local map and a travel book. I grabbed a coffee from the vending machine in the hotel lobby and headed out.

A crowd was gathered around a television in the Eurotel store, where I went to buy a new cell phone. I wanted to call my parents. I hadn't felt this homesick since my first summer at sleepaway camp when I was ten. After only two days, I'd begged my parents to take me home. Unbeknownst to me or my friend who'd suggested the camp, there were Shabbat services and morning prayers at breakfast. The forced religiosity got my hairs up, and I wrote a steady stream of letters home. "Get me out! They're making me thank God before I eat!" My parents promised it would get better, encouraging me to stay. And I suppose it did get somewhat better. I got the lead in the camp musical, *Hello, Dolly*. But it was a bribe and politically motivated. The camp didn't want me leaving early and sullying their clean attendance record. I went home early anyway. Goodbye, Dolly.

I joined the crowd that was watching a big-screen TV. A BBC news anchor reported four suicide attacks around London that had killed fifty-two people. It was devastating. My hotel could be next. Insurgents storming Hotel Pramen and detonating themselves in the lobby, sending black and white piano keys airborne. And then I thought, *What would be the point?*

After an hour setting up my cell phone with a non-English-speaking salesperson, I was off to get my monthly Metro card. It required a photo (new headshot?), so I searched for the photo booth that, according to my information folder, was inside a specific Metro station. The steep inclines of the escalators leading down into the underground stations were extraordinary. Some seemed to descend into the ninth circle of hell. I hopped on and off several trains and walked in several circles before I found the booth. Getting lost in a new city is inevitable, but it was incredibly annoying in 2005 before underground GPS. Also, my back muscles were spasming and I was dripping with sweat. I was hauling my laptop, too afraid to leave it at the hotel—the nonexistent windows and all.

I sat down in the photo booth and closed the curtain. It felt weird because I'd always associated photo booths with silly times with friends, lovers, or pets. You make funny faces, smooch, or make bunny ears behind someone's head. I gazed into the dot I believed to be the camera lens—I never knew where to look—and I pretended to be silly, like I was with my friend, lover, or pet. The strip of photos dropped down the shoot. I looked like I should've been on a flyer nailed to a tree: "Missing Adult. Warning: May Be Dangerous."

I headed to an expat internet café, Bohemian Bagel, looking for comfort food and my native language. On my way there, I passed the medieval Charles Bridge. Its numerous arches cut quite an impressive figure over the Vltava River. Apparently, it's one of Prague's most famous destinations.

"I'll have a tuna sandwich and a Turkish coffee, please."

The barista behind the counter wrote down my order and looked up. "Have you ever had a Turkish coffee?" she asked. "It's pretty intense."

"It's fine," I assured her. "I drink my coffee black." Did I look like someone who couldn't handle a cup of strong coffee?

Halfway in, the sludge ripped through me like a lit stick of dynamite. I hurried to the bathroom, making sure to avoid the barista. I wasn't in the mood for an "I told you so."

And then I couldn't figure out how to flush the damn toilet. I anxiously searched for a handle, a rope, or a foot pedal. I tiptoed out and made a beeline for a waitress. "Is there some special way to flush the toilet?" The waitress stared as if I'd asked her how to breathe. I returned to the bathroom, and after another round of pushing, pulling, hitting, and kicking, I leaned on the top of the tank lid— the whole lid depressed and the toilet flushed. Sneaky bastard.

Back at Hotel Pramen, I bumped into a young woman in the lobby who'd recently graduated from TEFL. I wanted feedback from someone other than Shelley, who was barely out of the Girl Scouts. No offense to the kid, but getting this young woman's reaction in the actual city felt more immediate and authentic. I was also hoping she would soothe some of my nerves.

"It was a tough month for sure," she said. "But I know I can teach English anywhere in the world now."

"Anywhere?" I playfully asked. "What about in the Serengeti?"

"Where?"

While brushing my teeth later that night, I turned over a thought in my head. For the most part, my ambitions and objectives in Los Angeles, where I was blissfully myopic and sealed off from the rest of the world, were a clear road. I knew where to go and what was required. Sure, there were sharp turns, bumps, and potholes along the way. But I always saw the road ahead. But this? This was off-roading. And I was afraid of losing traction and sinking into the mud.

I didn't recognize the person staring back at me in the cracked mirror above the bathroom sink. I'd been through many trying times in the past. But, as true as it was, right then, I couldn't think of one example.

My classmates and I sat at three long tables in the schoolroom. Our instructors, Paul and Timothy, introduced themselves. Paul was British, five foot eight and a hundred pounds soaking wet, with no ass. The circumference of both of his legs put together equaled one of mine. He wore an untidy pompadour, had a chipped front tooth, and owned 145 Rolling Stones albums—bootlegs and rare duets.

Timothy was thirty-nine, diminutive, with translucent skin and short blond hair. He was a father of two and said he'd been a forensics major at university. He might've been from the Midwest if it weren't for his Australian accent.

My fellow students took turns introducing themselves.

"Hi, my name is Jason," offered a bespeckled young man wearing board shorts and an Oxford button-down shirt. "From Miami originally. I just graduated from William and Mary with a degree in early childhood development. Psyched to be here."

"Hey, ya'll," said a pretty brunette sitting beside him, wearing an ill-fitting halter top. "I'm Cheryl." She giggled. "I just graduated—go Buckeyes—and tomorrow's my birthday. I'll be at The Drunken Monkey tonight. Come by." The class cheered. Not me. At her age, I'd run from bars and most social situations, too scared and insecure. Little has changed.

The stark age gap made my stomach twist. I had nearly twenty years on most of my classmates. I got crankier with every one of their scratchy yaps about the cheap local beer or announcements of "it's my first time in Europe!" It wasn't their fault. They were right on schedule. I was the impulsive idiot who'd closed her eyes and leapt without thinking. I was oblivious to see that this program might not be for someone of a certain age, who'd been married and divorced (a story for another time), with a living will in their safety deposit box. Someone who has a safety deposit box!

I genuinely wanted to teach, travel, and try something different. But honestly, I also moved to Prague because people told me how daring and cool it was—and therefore, I was. Ugh. Was there no end to my need for attention?

Timothy and Paul alternated leading the morning lessons, including hot topics like language awareness and teaching methodology. One morning in the program's first week, Timothy taught the class a few essential Czech words and then rambled about pronouns—I think they were pronouns. Before I signed up to teach English, I'd also failed to ask anyone if I needed to know more English grammar than a seventh grader. To be clear, I didn't. And I don't.

Timothy acted out a scene between two imaginary friends, turning his head from side to side to play both parts.

"Halo! Jak se máte?" (Hello! How are you?)

"Halo! Dobre. Jak se máte?" (Hello! Okay. How are you?)

"Dobre. Má jméno Robert. Co je tvůj jméno?" (Okay. My name is Robert. What's your name?)

"Má jméno Timothy." (My name is Timothy.)

I dug my thumbnail into my thigh to keep myself from laughing. Who could watch that with a straight face? I looked around the room, thinking, *This is hilarious, right? Who's with me? Jason? Cheryl?* No one was with me. They were as serious about the pronouns as Timothy.

We broke off into small groups to practice the friend exchange. I walked across the room and sat next to Tina and Randy, a married couple in their forties. They didn't seem to have a problem with the age difference. Their crow's feet and liver spots made me feel as dewy and ripe as a teenager.

"Jak se máte?" I asked Tina. She winced, and rightly so—I sounded like a nitwit.

I've never had an ear for languages. French classes in college were a nightmare. Even with extra tutoring, I sounded like a French toddler with a Bronx accent. However, it didn't stop me from spending a semester abroad in Paris. I attended the American College in Paris where classes were in English, but the French family I lived with insisted on only speaking French at home. Whenever I attempted a comment or asked a question in French, often during a meal, my heart raced, and my right cheek twitched.

"Veuillez passer le sel?" I'd ask Madame, butchering the words.

She'd shoot me a pompous smile. "Répétez, s'il vous plaît."

It was so tiring, and after only a week of constant repetition, I screamed, "Just pass me the goddamn salt." Well, I wanted to.

"Have you seen the MTV video of Mick Jagger and Tina Turner singing 'State of Shock'?" I asked Paul one afternoon.

He shook his head.

"Maybe the class can form a band. Wouldn't that be fun?!" I was dead serious. I imagined announcing my brilliant idea to my classmates. "Yes!" they'd agree. "Down with prepositions," they'd chant. "And dangling participles," I'd cry. "Let's put on a show!"

Paul smiled, but there was confusion in his eyes. He didn't know what to make of me or my suggestion. Now I was confused.

How could he not want to drop his life's work and transform TEFL into a school for the performing arts?

With the guarantee of travel as my new North Star, it was easy to ignore the required 130 hours of classroom learning that *was* the program. Instead of entertaining the possibility that I might have taken a wrong turn and walking away from the carnage, I'd try to save face by taking control and seeing if I could bend the school's curriculum to my will by forming a band (veering off the curriculum) and poking fun at Timothy's Czech survival class.

At the end of the first week, I taught two practice classes in front of live Czech students. Teaching alongside me were my fellow teachers in training Troy and Erin. Troy was a twentysomething snowboarder from Lake Tahoe. Erin was that girl in class who always forgot her notebook or umbrella, was seemingly careless, didn't study for tests—or so she said—and then got an A. I admired her, and I wanted her to fail.

I wrote my name on the whiteboard, and Vaclav, the first cute Czech boy I'd seen who also had all his teeth, laughed.

"Why are you laughing?" I asked, forgetting that he didn't speak English, which was why I was standing in front of the class in the first place. After a quick game of charades, I surmised that Dani was the name of his dog. I smiled. *Oh, Vaclav.*

When it was Troy's turn to lead, he handed out an article titled "Eat Your Heart Out in the USA." I thought it was too advanced, but I didn't say anything.

"What 'eat heart' mean?" asked Adéla, an adorable Czech grandmother.

"It means eating a lot," Troy answered.

Erin and I looked at each other, shaking our heads. *No, it doesn't.*

But we didn't argue because we'd lost interest. And it wouldn't have made any difference to Adéla.

Timothy sat in the back of the room, taking notes on our performances. When the last student left, he sat us down and gave us feedback. I was first.

"You did well, but you talked a bit too much," he said.

"Oh, okay." It wasn't the first time I'd heard this.

"It isn't actually the amount of talking," he clarified, "rather the amusing asides. They can confuse the students."

I sat up, grinning. *Amusing!* It'd been awhile since anyone found me amusing, and it felt great. Still, I waved it off. I was there to teach, not to be the class clown.

Class often consisted of making up stories based on photographs that we tore out of magazines. We'd practice communicating the descriptions. One afternoon, Timothy called on me. Forgetting where I was and the company I was in, I painted an expletive-filled and sexually inappropriate story. I wish I could remember what it was. The room fell silent, and I waited to be reprimanded—I'd definitely be summoned to the principal's office.

And then, everyone laughed. I'd almost forgotten what that sounded like. It would seem that I hadn't completely left performing behind. It'd hitched a ride to Prague.

"Dani," Timothy said, "teaching is wasted on you. You should be on TV."

Hold the phone! What are you saying? I shouldn't be a teacher? It was completely unexpected and came out of nowhere. I shifted in my seat, embarrassed. I wasn't looking for attention (honest). Almost immediately, I started wondering if Timothy's comment was proof that I shouldn't have left California. He reminded me of the part of myself that I'd quit. No. No matter how tempting it was, I would not be seduced by his comment. How many times can I pull myself up by my bootstraps without pulling my back out? His observation picked at my scab, and I was pissed. But I also wanted to believe that this pale Australian nerd who was passionate about education and who had probably never watched *Cagney & Lacey* knew what he was talking about. Still, even if he was right, what was I supposed to do about it? I didn't have a home in LA any longer. I didn't even own a coffee mug! Damn you, yard sale!

At the end of week two, Paul dropped the G-bomb in class.

"Each student," he announced, "will present a grammar lesson. It's a pass or fail." Flashes of every test I ever took, including pregnancy and driver's license, flooded in. I was terrified. I'm a horrible test-taker, and I know what I don't know.

I turned to Tina and Randy. Randy was flipping through an issue of *National Geographic* unbothered. "This is awful news. Nobody told me about this part."

Randy smiled. "You're a writer. It'll be a breeze." I failed to see the connection.

I found my name on the bulletin board once everyone had dispersed. I didn't want them to see me cry. The past perfect?! Why not just ask me to give a lesson on auctioneering—in American Sign Language?!

I knew it would be a long and stressful weekend of studying, so I walked to Tesco, a big-box grocery store, and stocked up on supplies. I was fond of their foot-long cheese baguettes smothered in a mysterious-tasting sauce that was the color of Silly Putty. I bought several—it was no time for healthy eating. I also tossed a couple packs of Petra cigarettes into my cart—it wasn't time to stop smoking, either. I'd started the revolting habit minutes after I landed in Prague. I was in Europe, and as I said, I didn't want to look like a tourist.

When I returned to my room, I set up my desk and laid out my papers, highlighters, and ashtray. I prepared for battle. I opened my textbook and read, "The past perfect, also called the pluperfect," and paused. Wasn't one name sufficient? I continued. "The past perfect is a verb tense used to talk about actions completed before some point in the past." What? I read the sentence three times and found an example: "We were shocked to discover that someone had graffitied 'Sara was here' on our garage door. We were relieved that Sara had used washable crayons."

The only thing that came from that example was a reminder of the time I got arrested for tagging an underpass in my hometown when I was a junior in high school.

I had no business explaining English to anyone, especially when I couldn't explain it to myself. This was Mr. Berman's fault— my seventh-grade English teacher. If he'd been paying attention, he never would've passed me. Perhaps my wicked acting chops and charming smile convinced him I understood what he was teaching.

I paced my room, lit a cigarette, and repeatedly read the definition and example out loud. Nothing.

On Saturday morning, I fanned out my papers across the floor to see if a different perspective would help. It didn't. I inhaled my third baguette. My head throbbed, and I felt nauseous. After several hours, I went for a walk around the building. I wouldn't allow myself to go to a movie or do anything fun. Nope, worrying was the surefire way of passing this test.

By Sunday night, I was drowning in dread and agitation. How could my future suddenly be dependent on explaining the past perfect? Either I'd pass and go on to teach the good people of Papua New Guinea, or I'd have to scramble for an alternate plan. It never occurred to me that teaching wouldn't work out. But I had to face the facts: Learning English grammar, never mind teaching it, had an expiration date, and mine had long passed.

"I'm leaving the program," I announced to Timothy and Paul in their office Monday morning. Failing here would've killed me. I imagined my family's reaction. They'd weep and shake their heads with the others in the search party behind Hotel Pramen. "It was the past perfect that killed her."

Timothy looked tearful. Paul was stunned. "It's just not happening, fellas," I said. "English is as foreign to me as it is to the Czechs. And, you said it yourself, Timothy—teaching is wasted on me." Served him right. He started it.

"It's true," Timothy said. "You've got TV. All I'm capable of is teaching."

What the hell was he talking about? I didn't have TV. I didn't have anything.

"English is your passion," I said, "as funny as that is." Timothy smiled, putting his chipped and gray teeth front and center. "Passion," I continued sincerely, "is the only thing that gets us out of bed in the morning." A platitude? About passion? That was rich.

They told me that Tina and Randy had dropped out two days earlier. Hearing this somehow justified my resignation and validated my theory that the program wasn't for grown adults.

I caught up with Tina and Randy later in the day and asked them why they'd left the program.

"We're travel agents," Tina explained. "Our time is better spent traveling, not sitting in a classroom."

"I hear that," I responded. Thankfully, they didn't press me for my reason.

I've had a lifetime of self-flagellation—pretty skilled at it. My parents rarely had to punish me when I was a kid. And on the rare occasion when I did need to be reprimanded, I'd usually take care of it myself. I'd send myself to my room and think about why I told my mom to "shut the hell up." Since I couldn't honor my teaching commitment, I felt I had to punish myself.

So, after quitting the program, I stayed in Hotel Pramen, where each night, tiny black and brown bugs gathered around the light fixture. They'd inch down the wall behind my head, edging closer to my ears. I swatted, squashed, and denied myself air-conditioning for several days. Also, thirteen dollars a night was hard to walk away from.

What to do, what to do? I couldn't go back to LA—it'd only been a few weeks since I left. How would it look? Friends threw parties for me. They gave me gifts and wrote sappy haikus about bliss, open roads, and sucking out the marrow of life. I'm sure one or two were even glad to see me go. It'd be mortifying to return so soon.

Before leaving, I'd also reconnected with three of my exes—not all simultaneously. I only initiated the reconnections because I knew I'd never see them again. Armed with an itinerary and a passport, I was free to decide where, when, and how my paramours and I rendezvoused, without any emotional attachment. It's not typically my go-to, but for one week in June 2005, I acted the part of a silver screen femme fatale. It'd be anticlimactic if I returned after such a Hollywood-worthy exit.

A few days later, when my punishment was over, I made a reservation at the Four Seasons Hotel. I needed a good night's sleep and toilet paper that didn't scrape my rectum. Before I left Hotel Pramen, I washed a few things in the sink, hung them up around the room to dry, and hoped the bugs wouldn't fly in and lay eggs in my socks.

The Four Seasons was one Metro stop away. I was ready to enter the station—my backpack on and a suitcase in each hand—and then I thought about all the stairs. I couldn't remember if there were elevators in the stations. The hotel was only one stop away, so I decided to walk. I was treating myself to a luxury hotel—I couldn't also take a cab. I rolled my suitcases over cobblestone streets, bobbing and weaving around summer tourists in 96-degree heat and 100 percent humidity. I'm confident that trek gave me a hernia.

"We've upgraded you to a king deluxe," said the hardy Irish man at reception. "However, the room isn't quite ready. Please help yourself to a cup of coffee in the lounge while you wait."

"Thank you." I'd gone from communism to capitalism in a matter of minutes.

The lounge was a comfortable seventy-one degrees, and the coffee had just the right amount of kick. I sat in a leather club chair and watched two small kids draw in coloring books on the floor.

"Is this your first time in Prague?" I asked the woman I assumed was their mother.

They were from Slovakia and on holiday. Overhearing my English and pegging me for an American, the kids, Dennis and Karin, popped up from the floor, screaming like recently adopted orphans. They asked if they could practice their English with me.

After reciting the alphabet, counting to fifty, and identifying body parts, I'd had enough. Of them. Of English. Of myself. I was happy to have helped, but I couldn't have cared less about the kids or their pronunciation.

I threw open the door to my room and collapsed on a puffy white cloud of yummy comforter. On one of the eighteen pillows shoved up against the headboard was a complimentary King Charles ball of chocolate. While unwrapping the gold foil, I turned over a small postcard. "*To prevent attracting the local wildlife, please turn off the lights when opening the window.*"

After an hour of caressing my face with the velvety hand towels and wiping my ass with plush, fifteen-ply toilet paper, I ran a bath. As much as I looked forward to soaking in the freestanding clawfoot tub, I couldn't relax. What was next? What was I going to do in the morning? Or the rest of my life? While I waited for the tub to fill, I sat on the edge and called Randy and Tina.

"Hey, Randy. Do you guys want to have lunch tomorrow? . . . No, I changed hotels . . . It's a long story."

Unfortunately, Randy and Tina were leaving the following morning for Riga, Latvia. Before we hung up, I asked them if they had any travel suggestions. But really, I just wanted to bury my head in a pillow and never leave.

Tina told me about their friend who sometimes worked with at-risk youths from disadvantaged neighborhoods in Nicaragua. "She's also a filmmaker. Maybe you can help in some way. Have you ever been to Central America?"

I set the phone in its cradle, opened the individual loofah, and slid under the bubbles. While attempting to smooth my cracked and callused heels (anything short of sandblasting was useless), my

Czech setbacks slowly evaporated. They were replaced by anticipation. I'd never been to Nicaragua. I wondered what their passport stamps looked like.

two

Mi Familia

THE TWO-INCH CIGARETTE ASH dangling from my dad's Parliament was dangerously close to falling into my lap. What was he waiting for? Flick it! Flick it! He wasn't paying attention and was definitely unconcerned about dirtying my new Sasson jeans.

It was the summer before my freshman year at NYU. We were sitting on the slippery green leather couch in our family room, hunched over yellow legal pads and studying a five-inch-thick course catalog. It was impossible to sit on that couch and not slide down to my neck. I suppose if I were sweaty, sticky, and unclothed, I might've stayed suctioned in place. But that would've been wrong, given whom I was sitting next to.

"What about Great Novels of the Enlightenment?" my dad asked.

"I don't know," I whined. "It sounds like a lot of reading."

He ignored me and stubbed out his cigarette in the ashtray on the coffee table.

"The History of the Universe?" he continued, not reading the room.

"That sounds overly ambitious." I wasn't about to tell him I had trouble remembering if the sun or the earth revolves around the other. And doesn't the moon do something? Instead, I started humming the words from the song "Across the Universe" by the Beatles.

I was accepted into the College of Arts and Science. Despite my experience, passion, and decade of preparation for a career on the stage, I was afraid to audition for a theater school. Something inside of me was falling apart—my confidence, maybe. The almost certain shame I'd feel if I didn't get in would've been unbearable. My guess is that the undoing began with the senior high school musical *Best Foot Forward*.

The auditions were open to all seniors, regardless of whether they had any experience in the theater or acting. I panicked. I mean, what was I dealing with? Who was my competition? The theater department had always been a close-knit group—a group with a pecking order. And by this time, I was perched on the top branch. Now, there were strangers and (I assumed) novices on my turf. I wondered if lacrosse star Scott McGrath or calculus phenom Tracy Morris could sing and dance. What if they had closeted musical theater aspirations? What if they were more talented than I thought I was? There was so much uncertainty. What if I only got a walk-on? Or a nonspeaking role? Or if I didn't get cast at all?!

So, just to be safe, I removed any and all chances of embarrassment and volunteered to be the stage manager. If you think about it, it was rather magnanimous of me. I was taking myself out of the running—relinquishing a spot to allow Scott or Tracy to experience the exhilaration of performing in front of a live audience and to feel the warmth of a spotlight on their face.

Wearing a headset and carrying a clipboard was a power I hadn't experienced before. I was the boss, calling the technical cues like an air traffic controller. And I liked it.

"House to half, go. Music intro one, go."

And if someone asked me why I wasn't applying to theater schools, I responded earnestly, "It's too limiting. Branching out into other areas like science and art history will make me more well-rounded as a performer." I convinced myself that learning the craft of acting was pretentious. Besides, my bigger dream was to be on television and in movies. And really, how much craft was involved in that?

It was easier to belittle what terrified me: being exposed as a phony whose only talent is that of a colossal know-it-all. So I shut the door on acting school and developed a boulder-size chip on my shoulder instead. I also wanted my dad's approval. Although he never said it out loud, I always felt that he feared having an idiot for a daughter or a daughter in theater school—or both.

Side note: I transferred to the film school in my sophomore year because I had no idea what to major in. Philosophy? Statistics? I laugh. I'd learn a "real" skill in film school—something tactile. And I didn't have to audition or make up stories or excuses.

"Dani, please turn off the television," my dad said without looking up from his legal pad.

The television had been on the whole time, but neither of us had noticed until that moment.

I ignored his request because I was distracted by the man on the screen. An older English gentleman was standing on a stage, addressing an audience. It was a lecture hall, just like the photos in the catalog. The man was wearing a bowtie and a white pocket square. Hefty bags under his eyes seemed to shake when he pounded a table with his fist, sending loose papers flying. Every so often, the camera cut away to close-ups of the students' faces. Some wrote furiously in their notebooks, others wiped beads of sweat from their forehead. Panic rippled up from my toes and settled in my chest.

"Oh, my God. Is that what college is going to be like?"

My dad turned around to see what I was looking at.

"First of all," he said, "I asked you to turn it off. And second, that's *The Paper Chase*—a fictional television show."

Maybe so, but it looked real to me.

"And in case you haven't noticed," he continued, "you're not going to Harvard Law School."

By my own admission, I was a television addict. And my addiction skewed my understanding and perceptions of the real world. And if people, such as my parents, assumed I could tell the difference, that's on them.

If a college course was offered titled, say, the Psychology of Hypocrisy, my family could be its research lab. I think it's safe to assume that one of the jobs of a parent is to shield their kids from negative influences, and making sure they aren't hanging out with predators and murderers. And what parent wants their kid to get a GED in a maximum-security prison? Also true is that parents model the behaviors they want their kids to emulate. They don't play in traffic, so their kids won't. My parents not only pushed me into traffic but also supplied the car that hit me.

The first time I fell under the television's spell, I was barely out of diapers. My parents bought my brother and me a thirteen-inch black-and-white Zenith television when we were five and four, respectively—they were the antithesis of helicopter parents, and they also couldn't afford a babysitter. They set the TV down on the oak dresser in the bedroom my brother and I shared in our apartment, plugged it in, adjusted the rabbit ears, and walked out. We didn't see them again until dinner days later.

My brother and I sat in front of the television every day—our tiny faces inches from the screen, as if we were reading a book. We'd squeal at the cartoons and sing along to commercial jingles. "*So always look for the union label; it says we're able to make it in the U.S.A.*"* I searched the back of the television for a portal where I could climb inside and join Laura Ingalls on the prairie. Trying to figure out how she and Pa got into our television was a real head-scratcher.

After weeks of watching dating game shows and human-sized puppets, and bolstered by my parents' benign neglect, I got hooked. I'd head straight into my bedroom after school, paw the hard plastic dial on the front panel, click it to the right, and wait for the TV to power up. Seeing the first image felt like getting shot with a tranquilizer dart.

Pretty soon, watching several hours a day wasn't enough. Prolonging the euphoria required more. How could I mainline John and Roy from *Emergency!* into my veins? I started faking stomach aches or sore throats to stay home from school so I could watch *Password*. My brother, on the other hand, had no problem turning the TV off after only ten minutes. He wasn't as hardcore as I was.

None of my friends in the neighborhood had TVs in their bedrooms. "But then, what do you do all day?" I asked. My heart ached

---

* From "Look for the Union Label" by Paula Green.

for them and their misfortune. So I invited them to hang out in my bedroom one afternoon—to get a taste. They got a bump of *Password*, and within minutes, we were playing along.

"Furrrrryyy?"

"Kitten!"

The street value of what I was offering? Priceless.

My behavior started to escalate. I picked fights with my parents and talked back to them—"Fuck off! You can't tell me what to do!"—so they'd think they were punishing me and send me to my room, where the television was.

And then my brother discovered *Star Trek*. His physical and mental transformation was frightening to watch. His pupils turned into big, hazel-colored saucers. His speech slurred, or out of nowhere, he'd scream, "*Khaaannn!*" I didn't know what the hell he was saying. I didn't watch *Star Trek*—it was too unrealistic for me. But I knew he was riding the wave. Two addicts in a tiny room wasn't sustainable, and we argued constantly. However, my brother and I were sober enough to know that our parents could take the television away at any time if they wanted to.

One afternoon, while watching the only show we could agree on, *Barney Miller*, the picture started flickering. I stood on my chair and reached for the antenna. When I sat back down, my brother, thinking it would be funny, pulled the chair out from underneath me. The Zenith fell onto my right leg, breaking it in two places—my leg, not the TV, although it too was shattered. And that was that.

Detoxing was full of wild cravings and hallucinations. My brother and I proved that we could quit if we had to. But luckily, we didn't have to. Six months later, we moved into a house with separate bedrooms, and our dealers hooked us up with our own televisions.

The Paper Chase was fiction. I got it, eventually, but John Houseman wasn't the only thing that scared me about going to college in the city. That summer, before I left for school, I saw the film *Prizzi's Honor*, about the mafia and assassins in Brooklyn—which, in my mind, wasn't far from the Washington Square Arch.

I'd seen the mafia on the evening news and in the papers, and now I was going to school in the mob's backyard. Anyone and everyone were a target. What chance did I have? What would stop Sammy the Bull from taking me out while I roller-skated under the arch? I was walking right into the lion's den.

The morning of move-in day, my dad threw my suitcases into the trunk of our gray Volvo station wagon. He and my mom got in the front seat, and I climbed into the back. My mom took out her latest knitting project and turned on her favorite country music station. As a friend said to me years later, "Even cowgirls can be Jews." I leaned my head against the window, with my cheek pressed up against the glass. *How am I supposed to feel safe? What are the authorities doing to stop the blood from flooding the Manhattan streets? Why aren't my parents concerned? Maybe I should commute.*

It wasn't my parents who insisted I go to school in Manhattan. I had to be in New York City—the big talker that I was. I'd also brought this worry on myself—and with good reason. I had first-hand experience with gangs.

Back in my childhood apartment, when the Zenith died, I desperately wanted something to do. So I'd asked a few badass third and fourth graders in the neighborhood if I could join their gang. I'd supplied them with the narcotic in my bedroom, so, yeah, they owed me.

We wore denim bell bottoms, leather vests, and Puma Clydes. I was the only one in pigtails—which got me the nickname Pigtails.

We roamed the streets like the kids in the gangster musical *Bugsy Malone*, only without the prepubescent showgirls and Paul Williams soundtrack. I tried (oh, how I tried) to convince Olivia to add some singing and dancing to our roaming, but she wouldn't have it. She said it would stain our credibility.

Olivia Dominguez was our fierce leader. She was a rebel and, at ten years old, the wise elder of the group. We followed her wherever she wanted and did whatever she asked. We kicked around abandoned beer bottles lying in the gutters or searched beside garbage cans for discarded cigarette butts, hoping to find one that might allow for a drag or two. I refused to smoke the lipsticky ones. We loitered in lobbies of office buildings and sometimes asked random people for change. If we got hungry, we hit the aisles of the A&P and squirted Easy Cheese into each other's mouths. Maybe I'm boasting, but if you saw us strutting around the neighborhood, you'd definitely want to be one of us.

My parents were oblivious to what I was doing, who I was hanging out with, or my whereabouts most afternoons. They were just glad that I was sleeping straight through the night without crying out for Maude.

One day, after terrorizing street signs by pelting them with rocks, Olivia decided she and the others were walking me home. The sun was setting and it was almost dinnertime. I thought it was a sweet gesture, if uncharacteristic. We arrived at my apartment building, a six-story red-brick structure, and they walked with me to the back entrance. I thanked everyone for making sure I got home safely, and I started down the concrete steps leading to the heavy metal door and the elevators. The next thing I knew, Olivia grabbed me by the shoulders and pushed me back against the wall. The others instantly formed a barricade on either side of her—a human fence in case I fought back or tried to run.

Mi familia had betrayed me.

Olivia removed a knife from the inside of her vest and slowly and confidently unfolded the blade from the handle. It was probably only two inches long, but I saw a machete. She held the edge to my neck, delicately indenting my skin, teasing. I was in shock. No one stepped forward to help me. They just stared at Olivia. She was holding me hostage. I wondered if she'd call my parents and demand a ransom. What could she get on the black market for a nine-year-old TV junkie? My parents weren't wealthy—how high would they go? Would they even hear the phone ringing over my dad's bongo drumming that he'd recently taken up? I had 50 cents in my pocket. I could offer it to Olivia along with my yo-yo. It would've been a bummer, though. I'd finally learned how to do the trick around the world without giving myself a black eye.

I thought maybe Olivia was testing me—to see how tough I was. I'd given her a bump of *Petticoat Junction*; maybe she didn't think that was gritty or edgy. And now, Olivia was about to see my quivering jelly insides.

It didn't make sense. We'd hung out in her apartment the day before. It was only the second time I'd been in her home. Her brother Max was creepy, and so was their apartment. One entire wall was devoted to terrariums of snakes. There were twenty or more piled on top of one another. I'd think they were running a pet store if I didn't know any better.

The first time I went over to Olivia's, Max took one of his snakes out of its enclosure and held it up to my face, bullying me. "Here, hold it. Go on, hold it. You're not scared, are you?" I wanted to bolt out of the room. But I couldn't. I had to stand my ground, even if it meant peeing a little in my pants.

"Nah, not interested," I said without flinching, fighting back tears.

After I rebuffed Max, Olivia grabbed something from underneath her mattress.

"Here." It was the book *Forever* by Judy Blume. "Don't tell anyone where you got it."

"Why?" I asked. She handed me the book as if it were a baby Gibbon smuggled in from India.

"Read it. You'll see. And don't forget to give it back to me when you're finished."

I stuffed the book into the waistband of my pants.

Skipping down the hill to my apartment later that afternoon, I wondered why I never saw Olivia's parents. And I assumed that she and Max were orphans. It would explain why Max was allowed to have so many pet snakes and keep Tupperware containers of mice in the refrigerator.

Wait! I screamed to myself, careful not to make any sudden moves and risk a beheading. *Was she holding me hostage because I hadn't returned the book?* I was about to explain that I was a very slow reader, but before I opened my mouth, Olivia lowered her knife, folded it, slid it back inside her suede vest, and smiled at me. I matched her smile and raised her a soft chuckle, letting her know I was in on the prank.

No one ever brought up the incident again. Nor did I tell my parents what happened. I wanted to ensure I lived long enough to see the fifth grade.

I'd calmed down considerably by the time we got on the FDR

Drive. Reliving the story about Olivia soothed my nerves. If I could walk away from snakes and machetes, I could hold my own against the Genovese and Colombo families.

My parents helped me unpack my suitcases in my dorm room. My mom made my bed, and we said goodbye. None of it was a big deal. I was only fifty minutes from home, and we'd already made plans to have dinner the following night. I hung a few posters around my meager wall space—the John Travolta–Jamie Lee Curtis tour de force *Perfect*, Barbara Streisand's 1983 *Life* magazine cover. I plugged in my phone and answering machine.

While recording my outgoing message, I heard the door open. It was one of my roommates, Cynthia.

"Oh, hi," I said, greeting her.

"Hi. It's nice to finally meet you. I hope you don't mind," Cynthia said, pointing to a brand new seventeen-inch color beauty still in the box and a stack of *Quiet Riot* albums. They were strapped together on a hand truck. The Lord giveth, and the Lord taketh away.

I hadn't brought my TV to school because I thought it was time to go cold turkey and dry out. As a college student, I assumed that I'd be too busy to watch television, what with all the lectures, homework, and studying that I'd be doing.

Cynthia and I talked while she unpacked. After ten minutes, she went downstairs to dinner with her parents before they drove back to Kentucky. I lay on my bed and recorded different outgoing messages. "Please leave me a message when you hear the beep. Or the tone." My nose started to run, and my skin felt clammy and itchy. The pull was just too strong, and I couldn't resist. I stood up from my bed and slowly approached the television.

I had a new pusher, and her name was Cynthia. I was back using and abusing later that night.

P.S. There's always time to watch television. You just have to want it bad enough.

three

Bathrooms Without Borders

WHEN I WAS GROWING UP, my two best friends and I never talked about getting married or having kids. I don't recall us ever playing house or making a list of our favorite baby names. Although, if I had, mine definitely would've included Ethel and Wednesday—obviously. Instead, we got dropped off at the local mall and shoplifted keychains and baseball hats at the Denim Mine. Or we'd have sleepovers and order a half dozen pizzas to be delivered to the homes of girls we didn't like in our middle school. Sorry, Veronica.

When we were older, we graduated to reenacting whatever music video was popular at the time, like Madonna's "Like a Virgin" and Whitesnake's "Here I Go Again." We considered all of Charlie's Angels to be role models—real independent career women. We imagined riding motorcycles and having affairs with dark-haired and dangerous-looking men that we picked up in smoky European cafés. We would travel the world and have big, important lives. I just assumed we'd all eschew anything that remotely smelled of domesticity or conventional institutions, like marriage and motherhood.

Then, in our late twenties, we all got married.

After six years of marriage, however, I remembered that I never wanted to be married and got divorced. I did remain child-free. So, in this respect, I stayed faithful to myself and my early promises. And while my best friends also divorced, they both had kids. Traitors!

But I didn't get to sit on my high horse for long. Many years after my divorce, when I was cozying up to forty, I was stricken by amnesia (again) and committed treason against myself. (Is that even a thing?)

I was seduced by Julian, a divorced dad right out of the pages of an erotic airport romance novel. And even though his kids, thirteen-year-old Nicole and nine-year-old Tyler, were a part of the package, I moved in with him anyway. I didn't birth the kids, so it wasn't like I went back on my word, as my friends had. But there were many moments after unpacking my toiletries and cutlery when I wondered, *What the hell am I doing with kids in my life—and in New Jersey?*

That's dumb love for ya.

As far as kids go, Tyler and Nicole were easy, and they consistently surprised me—for the better. Whenever I expected Tyler to throw a tantrum because he didn't get his way or morph into a devil child rejecting his dad's new girlfriend, he didn't. Instead, he'd ask me to toss a ball around like I was one of his playmates. My guard was always up around Nicole, though, at least in the beginning. She was an aggressive and self-possessed teenager with an attitude—that's the most intimidating kind. And yet she accepted me outright and unconditionally.

Admittedly, I was a real pill those first few custodial weekends. I thought Nicole and Tyler would be more in the background. And I didn't think having the kids around would be all that difficult or intrusive. Besides, they weren't my responsibility; I wasn't expected to discipline them. I'd hang out backstage and watch the show. Still, it didn't take much—a soccer game here, Christmas tree shopping there—to make me feel annoyingly put upon.

It became increasingly evident that if Julian and I were going to make it to our golden years, I was going to have to embrace his kids and take more of a hands-on approach. Okay, sure. But exactly how I would accomplish this wasn't entirely clear.

Julian's dynamic with Nicole and Tyler didn't look like the one I grew up with. He didn't ask Nicole philosophical questions like my dad had asked me at her age. "What do you think Sartre meant when he said, 'Hell is other people'?" As far as I could tell, the kids weren't being exposed to music masterpieces or great works of literature or art. Why hadn't Julian taken them to the ballet or the opera like my parents had with me? Wasn't it in their best interest? Let me stop right here and say that the cultural shit only happened when my parents realized that the boob tube monster they'd created was a direct reflection on them and were now trying to undo some of that damage.

Nicole and Tyler were smart and intuitive. And they knew how lucky they were to have someone like me around. I'd ensure that they got a dose of *Madame Bovary* and *Aida*. And as a bonus, I'd get on them about using "like" and "ya know" when they spoke so they didn't sound ignorant—like my parents had done with me. Boy, were those kids lucky to have me.

After about a year, the four of us fell into a nice rhythm. I surprised myself with how accepting and welcoming I was, bringing

Tyler and Nicole into my life. The weekends became something I looked forward to and not an obligation. Maybe my friends were onto something. It was a chance to bond when I drove Tyler to ice hockey practice or wherever. I taught him about improvisational comedy. And he educated me on the latest (and most explicit) hip-hop songs. Nicole often confided in me about boyfriends and bitchy classmates. The real ego boost came when she asked me to show her how to pump her own gas. I stayed open and paid close attention to the moments when I genuinely enjoyed playing the girlfriend-mom-like role. And whenever I was given the chance, I relished telling the kids what to do.

When Nicole was eighteen and on a break from college, she spent a weekend with us. I was working out and preparing for a Pilates class I was teaching that evening. About a year after Julian and I started dating, we broke up for a while. I was crushed. Writing—a solitary and lonely endeavor to begin with—became excruciating after heartbreak. I'd thought about becoming a Pilates instructor in the past as a side gig, but it'd never worked out. By the time Julian and I got back together nine months later, I'd given birth to a Pilates career—in addition to my other careers.

I was in the home gym on the third floor next to Julian's loft-style office.

Nicole yelled from the primary bedroom on the second floor, "Can I borrow a movie?" The DVDs lived on a shelf over the dresser.

"Take whatever you want," I hollered back.

While I was studying Pilates and grieving our breakup, Julian bought a piece of property where he could build his dream beach house. I wasn't interested in taking on the hassle and effort. But I was in love, and I committed to my new home life. However, the house never truly felt like mine or ours. I often felt like an interloper whenever I offered my opinion or suggested decorating choices.

Some of Julian's design ideas, like in our bedroom, were really unusual. He wanted the bathroom to be an open layout, where the shower, bathtub, and toilet were essentially in the bedroom, like a bathroom without borders. He argued that a bathroom door was unnecessary because the toilet sat behind a half wall. I urged him to reconsider, remarking, "Some of us like a little mystery." While lying in bed, I could simultaneously watch *The Today Show* and Julian shaving his behind. Watching him soap his man parts was often erotic, although I could've done without the manscaping while I watched Lester Holt's report on U.S. combat operations in Iraq.

Julian and I were oceans apart when it came to privacy. I required ample amounts, while Julian barely wanted any. When I found out that he told Nicole what birth control I used, I nearly threw a fit. And when I confronted him, Julian didn't understand why I was throwing said fit. He didn't get it even when I tried to explain that I didn't think it was his place to share my personal information. I didn't have the strength to continue pleading my case, so I dropped it.

I'd also swallowed my concerns when Julian told me Tyler had found our lube.

"What do you mean he found it?" I'd asked.

I couldn't imagine we'd forgotten it on the chaise lounge on the deck. Could we have left it on the kitchen counter, lying between the Muslim man and woman salt and pepper shakers I'd brought back from Dubai? The lube typically lived in Julian's nightstand, where most people keep their lube. (I don't mean that most people's lubes are in Julian's nightstand specifically—I assume they'd be in their own nightstands.)

Julian said that Tyler asked what it was used for. To be fair, it would've elicited questions from anyone—it was called Gun Oil and packaged in the shape of a large brown bullet.

Clearly, Tyler had been snooping. But instead of reprimanding him for invading our privacy in a TV-worthy father-son fireside chat, Julian told Tyler that the Gun Oil was to lubricate door hinges.

I rolled my eyes and walked away.

Nicole hollered out several movie titles, asking me for recommendations. And then Julian shouted from the kitchen, "I'm going up to shower, and then I'll make us lunch."

I stopped midway through a push-up, calculating. *While Nicole is going through DVDs in our bedroom, is Julian going to disrobe and step into the shower in the see-through glass stall—also in the bedroom?* I imagined him lathering and loofah-ing, carefree and oblivious, while Nicole tried to decide between *Something's Gotta Give* and *The Help*. *What if she sees her dad naked?* The blood drained from my face.

My parents sometimes walked around the house in their underwear until I was probably ten. And then they had the decency to cover up. I never wanted to see my mom loading the dishwasher wearing only her bra and thong or my dad emptying the dishwasher in tighty-whities. And if that makes me a prude, then make me a T-shirt. I will wear it proudly.

Nicole shouted again. "Have you seen *Lincoln*?"

I sprang up from my yoga mat. "I loved it," I screamed. Why was Nicole still in the bedroom? The acoustics in the house were such that no matter where you were, you could hear what was happening in every other room. If I heard Julian's bathing announcement, I figured so did she. But even if she didn't, I assumed Julian would tell her to leave when he saw her.

The house was still.

I told myself that what was happening at that moment wasn't anything to clench about. But I had my doubts. Parents don't take showers in front of—or with—their kids after a certain age, right? I held on to this belief. Accepting the kids into my life was one thing. But there was no way I'd stick around if it were acceptable practice for Julian and Nicole—who, might I remind you, was eighteen at this point—to shower together or be in the room when the other was showering.

I flashed back to when I was nine and my family moved from our apartment in New York to the house in suburbia. The only upside to moving was getting my own room. Now, I could dance around in my leg warmers while writing angsty teenage poetry in peace. One night, quite late, something set off the security alarm. Loud and obnoxious beeping pounded throughout the house, shaking the walls. It could only mean one thing—an intruder was about to beat me and my family to death with a hammer. Our bloodied bodies wouldn't be discovered until the neighbors wheeled their trash bins to the end of their driveways on garbage day and smelled rotting flesh coming from next door.

I jumped up from my captain's bed, tiptoed across the chocolate-brown shag rug, and cracked open my door. I heard mumbling voices and doors slamming coming from my parents' bedroom at the far end of the hall. As scared as I was, I didn't run to them. What if I wasn't fast enough? I'd be the first one put down.

My parents turned off the alarm before I lost all of my hearing. And then, walking toward my room at the top of the staircase, was

Dad, wearing nothing but a pair of red, nut-hugging bikini briefs—
tight enough to see his manhood. He had a rifle—a BB gun rifle,
I'd later learn—slung across his hairy chest. I was both queasy and
curious. *Why did we have a rifle in the house? And were all men that
hairy?* He looked like the cover model for the porn version of *American
Rifleman* magazine. There isn't enough therapy in the world to
erase that image.

My dad went downstairs, I assumed to confront the intruders.
I went back into my room and collapsed onto my bed. I don't know
what was more terrifying, my dad in his banana hammock or the
possibility of being massacred.

Back in the home gym, I chewed my cuticles and paced the
floor mats like an expectant father in a hospital waiting room circa
1956. I heard faint sounds of running water coming from the bathroom. I froze. *Is Julian getting in the shower while Nicole looks on?*
What was I missing? In my gut, I knew what was right and what
might be considered objectionable behavior. But I second-guessed
myself. I wasn't Nicole's mother or a parent. How could I know if
this didn't happen in other families? Maybe it's some progressive
hippy-dippy shit. Maybe it was a European thing—Julian is Portuguese. Wait, my dad is half Lithuanian. Hmm.

"Nicole, put down *J. Edgar* and get the hell out of there! Julian,
this isn't Lisbon!" That's what I would've screamed had I not been
too stunned to open my mouth.

Someone had to protect Nicole from a potential run-in with
her own nut-hugger-wearing father—or worse. I may not have been
her mom, but I still thought it was my job to keep Nicole safe.
But what if I was overstepping? Was I overreacting? Being childish?
What if this freakout was because of my own issues? (See above.)

Going along with the construction of a house was a far cry from going along with whatever may or may not have been happening one flight below. I had to see and stop *it* if needed.

I walked into Julian's office, a loft that looked over our bedroom. I couldn't see the shower. So I folded my upper body over the cold iron railing of the spiral staircase that led down to the bedroom/bathroom. My waist pressed into the rods for support while I craned my neck for a better angle. I extended my body farther and farther until my feet floated off the ground.

At that moment, I swore off TV procedural crime dramas. All they do is encourage paranoia and mistrust. Every seemingly harmless and casual act (like driving a kid to school) becomes an unimaginable crime or lecherous felony. Every stock trader and nun is a suspect.

Was inadvertently getting a peek at your dad's junk the worst thing in the world? No one was calling it pleasant, but was stopping it worth impaling myself? "Next, on *48 Hours*: Rattled girlfriend mom falls to her death because of her overactive imagination."

I was pretty sure Nicole and Tyler's biological mom would never dangle over a third-floor railing to spy on her family. Meanwhile, I was scared and too embarrassed to walk into the bedroom and confront my lover and his daughter. But what actually stopped me was the possibility of shaming Nicole and Julian. It wouldn't have scored me any points. And what would I even say if my suspicions were correct? I didn't have that speech cued up and ready to go.

While thinking about my next move, which I'd hoped included getting the feeling back in my thighs, I saw Nicole balancing a stack of DVDs in her arms. *What the hell?* Was she hosting a film festival in the den? She casually walked out of the bedroom and closed the door. I exhaled. I'd been holding my breath for the past ten minutes. My feet hit the floor, and the color returned to my face.

I immediately rang my friend Diane and told her what had happened. I needed an objective opinion.

"Do you think anything improper went on?" Diane asked.

"No." My defensive tone indicated otherwise. Why else would I have called her? Still, I wished she hadn't been so direct—it made the whole incident sound even more salacious.

"It was probably cultural or an innocent lapse of judgment."

Julian had a laissez-faire (or whatever the Portuguese equivalent is) approach to most things—nudity, schooling, parenting. Although, he'd also been on American soil for decades. What was the statute of limitations on using one's European roots as an excuse? I decided to go with lapse of judgment.

At the bathroom sink that night, I washed my mouthguard, and Julian brushed his teeth.

"That was kind of weird," I said, "the whole shower thing with you and Nicole." I hoped my lighthearted approach would disarm him. "I mean, why didn't she leave when she saw you?"

I threw Nicole under the bus because it was more important that Julian didn't think I was criticizing his parenting skills, which I was.

Julian screwed the cap back on the toothpaste. "Yeah, it was kind of weird," he agreed. "I didn't know what to say. What was I going to do?" He sounded sensitive and clueless. But if he didn't know how to handle something like this, where did that leave me?

"Maybe we could talk to Nicole," I suggested. "We can explain why this made me uneasy." Theoretically, it sounded like a good idea—to clear the air and set some boundaries. But practically, it would undoubtedly be embarrassing for everyone—especially me. "It's not necessary. It's over." Julian turned away from the sink and walked across the room to the bed, dragging his feet like he was scraping mud off the bottoms of his slippers. *How lazy do you have to be not to lift your feet when you walk?*

I slid under the sheets next to him. I couldn't let it go, and we took turns defending our positions. Ultimately, they were Julian's kids, and it was his call. But refusing to back me up and talk to Nicole was really crappy. Julian had put me in an awkward position. His attitude made me consider the very real possibility of ending the relationship. I actually started packing my bags in my head. I tried recalling every item in the house that was mine so I wouldn't forget to pack it. How could our relationship survive if I couldn't express myself and have my feelings taken seriously? I'd put in my time, goddamn it.

Nicole and I went to dinner at a neighborhood Thai restaurant a few days later. It was the first time we'd gone out together alone. I planned to talk to her about what had happened. As we nibbled on khao pad, I struggled to find the words. How could I satisfy my need to be heard and have my values respected while also not making Nicole uncomfortable? After several forkfuls, my anticipation became unmanageable. I figured if I just started to talk, then eventually something I said would make sense.

"So, well, sometimes you or Tyler do things that make me uptight," I said. "And I'd like you guys to know that."

Nicole looked up from the pineapple curry bowl. "Uh huh."

"Being in the bathroom with your father while he's . . . it was awkward," I continued. "You didn't do anything wrong—at all. I just don't think it's appropriate. I'm not being unreasonable, am I?" I wanted to finesse my grievance, but I blathered on ungracefully.

"My parents walked around the house naked all the time growing up," Nicole offered. "It wasn't a big deal." I suppose that was helpful information, and it gave me context, but now I'd forever have that visual swimming around in my head.

"I get it," I said. "I grew up in a sometimes-naked household as well." No, I hadn't. But I wanted Nicole to know that I understood, so I regaled her with my rifle-toting porn-model dad story.

Nicole laughed. But her tone sounded more like pity.

"You're older now, and I just don't think . . . because it's different in our house. It's complicated. I mean, I'm not your mom, and you're not my kid . . ." As soon as I said it, I stopped talking. I meant to speak honestly, but it was like walking a tightrope, trying to protect her feelings while caring for my own.

I tried to read her expression. *How* ABC Afterschool Special *did I sound?*

Nicole nodded. "You're right."

"I am?"

"Yeah, it was inappropriate."

Yay me.

Nicole told me that when she saw her dad turn on the water in the shower, she left the room, avoiding any glimpses. She knew.

After Nicole's affirmation, I felt more confident in my role. I was practically an expert now, which is why I wrote an entire book about being a girlfriend mom.

"By the way," Nicole said, laughing, "I found your glass dildo."

"Not again!"

"Uh, I'll come back a little later." It was our waiter. I hadn't seen this poor soul standing behind me.

Tyler had absconded with the vibrator in question a couple of months earlier. What was it with these two?

I'd caught Tyler standing in front of my nightstand, holding my black velvet pleasure pouch with the top of my glass dildo sticking out. Again, I'd been in the loft, looking down at the action. My heart beat in triple time. How could this sweet boy I'd carved pumpkins with and who'd noticed the new hand soap I put in the bathroom be the thief I was staring at?

"Tyler!" I hadn't intended to scream his name as if he were dangling a baby over the balcony of a burning building. It was a knee-jerk reaction. Tyler couldn't make out where the bloodcurdling cry had come from, so I screamed again, confident that the next-door neighbors were dialing 911. This time, Tyler ran out of the bedroom with the dildo bobbing up and down in the pouch. I bolted down the staircase, careful not to slip, hit my head, and die, which at that point would've been my preference.

"Tyler, please come back here." He didn't. What was he thinking? That he'd rummage through the pouch in his bedroom, take inventory, and return it when the coast was clear?

I walked into the hall just as Tyler emerged from his bathroom, giving me a look like, "What's all the yelling about?"

"Can I have it, please?" I squeaked. I hoped he knew what "it" was because I didn't want to say "pleasure pouch" out loud. Without uttering a word, he grabbed the pouch from the bathroom sink and handed it to me like we were undercover drug dealers. As unbearable as the event was, I didn't want to make him feel self-conscious for being curious just because I was trembling like an earthquake aftershock.

"Can you tell me why you took it?"

Tyler averted his eyes and shrugged, signaling the end of the conversation. We walked away in opposite directions.

Minutes later, Julian found me circling an armchair in our bedroom. And when I asked him if he'd heard me screaming, he said, "I thought you and Tyler were kidding around." Either way, why not investigate just to be sure? I told Julian what had happened, and he was at a loss for words. Rare. Not so rare was his request to simply forget it. So I decided to take matters into my own hands.

I found Tyler in the living room playing on his phone as if he hadn't had a glass dildo in his hands twenty minutes earlier. I sat on the coffee table, took a deep breath, and stared at him.

"I'm sorry I screamed like a maniac. But that's my personal property. You don't belong in anyone's drawers but your own unless you have permission to be there." Tyler didn't dismiss what I was saying with a grunt or wave me off with some moody teenage attitude. So I prattled on. "Sneaking around and taking what's not yours isn't okay." I'm surprised I didn't add "honesty is the best policy" and "crime doesn't pay."

I asked Tyler again why he took the pouch. He said he was looking for my phone charger, which I usually keep on my nightstand. And when it wasn't there, he opened the drawer, saw the pouch, and wanted to see what was inside. I asked if he had any questions about what he saw. He was quiet for a moment and then grinned, revealing a mouth full of metal.

Thank you, Tyler, for not having any questions.

From then on, I kept my phone charger in plain sight, and Mr. Glass was never mentioned again in mixed company. As embarrassing as it was for me to talk to Tyler, it also connected us—like we were the only two survivors of a plane crash.

"You're so easy," Nicole said, getting up from the table and putting on her jacket. "Tyler and I purposely do things because we know how you'll react. It's fuckin' funny."

I reached across the table and gently touched Nicole's arm. "So then you *didn't* find it?"

I forgive my friends for changing their minds and having kids—we all make mistakes. And I also understand their choices. I delighted in being a girlfriend mom for much of the time Julian and I were together. But deep down, I always knew that the role was temporary. It was like wearing a Halloween costume and playing make-believe. Eventually, I took off the disguise and was left with my original intent—first, straddling the hood of my car like Tawny Kitaen and then walking alone, like a drifter, just as it was meant to be.

four

Celebrity Adjacent

IN 1998, MY THEN HUSBAND and I lived in an area in Los Angeles known to the locals as Beverly Hills adjacent. Funnily enough, adjacent also summed up my life at the time. I seemed to always be next to the big break or near the successful friend. My husband was a struggling musician—because two dreamers with inflated and fragile egos in a house are better than one, right? There were many, many hopeless and unspectacular years.

My husband was extremely talented. He could play whatever instrument he put his hands on. When we were first married, I envisioned us becoming a variety act, going on tour, and then breaking up over creative differences. We had the talent and the microphones. Unfortunately, my husband didn't share my vision. Denying me the chance to give the world another power couple in the world of entertainment was a personal affront. It took me a long time to get over it and stop blaming him for my adjacent status.

After several unsuccessful musical partnerships, my husband put out an ad in *Music Connection*, a trade magazine, looking for collaborators.

Enter Amy and Kelly, professional musicians and lifelong friends. When they came to our apartment to meet my husband, I invited myself into the meeting. The four of us hit it off immediately. Physically and vocally, Kelly reminded me of Olivia Newton-John. She had the same angelic and breathy voice and a ridiculous vocal range. It made me think about singing and my fifth-grade chorus snub. I would've given my liver for Kelly's pipes.

If Joan Jett and Lou Reed had a love child, that was Amy—all punk and grunge, with a fiery mop of long, curly red hair. When she sang, she was aggressive, emotional, and raw. But when she wasn't singing, she was shy and unassuming. I admired her ability to switch back and forth. Kelly and Amy had been friends since nursery school. They finished each other's sentences and knew what the other was thinking. It was like watching twins interacting with one another. They were both wicked talented, and I wanted to be friends.

At that first meeting, my husband and Amy picked up a couple of acoustic guitars and started to play. They watched each other's fingers pick and pluck, improvising melodies. The collaboration had begun. And I was envious. I thought about the piano lessons my parents forced me to take when I was nine and how I rebelled against practicing. "You can't tell me what to do!" It's a regret that keeps on giving.

Not long after we'd met, we were all sitting around my dining room table when Amy casually tossed a grenade on the conversation. She said that she was in a band with Chastity Bono. That by itself was a real doozy. But then the grenade exploded when she announced that she and Kelly were friends with Cher.

Anyone who knows me knows that I was slightly fixated on Cher when I was young. I'd fantasize about sharing a stage with her, singing duets lying side by side on the top of her upright piano, being adored by millions, and replacing Chastity as her daughter. When my friends came over to play, I often suggested that we act out sketches from *The Sonny and Cher Comedy Hour*. It wasn't as popular an idea as I'd thought. Performing comedy sketches was a lot to ask of them—I see that now.

Surely, I didn't feel the same way about Cher anymore. As an adult, I'd matured, and things had changed. That was my assumption, anyway. However, Amy's revelation transported me right back to 1971. I didn't know how to react to this new information. How could I have when I'd never imagined someone with Amy's connections coming into my life, let alone into my apartment?

What were the chances that the only person who answered my husband's ad was the person who could (potentially) deliver me to Cher? This had to be some karmic destiny. The showbiz goddesses were rewarding me for decades of unfailing loyalty to the dark lady when everyone else was listening to Pink Floyd and watching *Star Wars*.

I was Cher adjacent!

And close to the fire. If I didn't keep my enthusiasm and imagination under wraps, someone (likely me) would get burned. Pretending that this wasn't the most remarkable turn of events would require a lot of acting—and I'm not that good.

I took a deep breath. "Do you have Cher's phone number?" I asked Amy. "Personal email?" I couldn't tell if Amy's and Kelly's glares were ones of kindness or fear. I was trying to sound like I was joking. But I had to know. I held my breath, waiting for the answers.

"Yeah. Why?" Amy asked as she took a hit off her joint.

"No reason. Just curious." Amy didn't pursue my line of questioning, which was a relief. I couldn't convey the big deal-ness of the info—not yet, anyway.

The girls were no longer just talented musicians. They were the gatekeepers. They possessed a superpower—a personal relationship with someone who had meant so much to me as a kid. Sometimes, it felt like they lorded it over me, teasing me. It was insufferable to hear about their Sunday brunches at Geoffrey's in ordinary terms. Or their invitations to sit in on Cher's recording sessions. My proximity to their critical proximity made me sweat whenever I was around them. I hoped when I asked questions like "Where does Cher bank?" or "What brand of toothpaste does she use?" it came off as casual and innocuous.

The last thing I wanted was for Amy and Kelly to think I was using them as pawns in my master plan to rendezvous with Cher, because I genuinely liked them. I would've been their friend even without their connection. But it was definitely a bonus.

In a short time, I forged a close and intimate relationship with the girls. Amy talked openly about her brief stint in the military. And Kelly was only too happy to share details of her sex life with her fireman boyfriend. It was only fair that I came clean.

One night, after a rehearsal in our apartment, I sat them down in our living room.

"There's really no easy way to say this," I began. "So I'm just going to say it."

My husband took a swig of his Heineken. He knew what was coming and he steadied himself.

"For as long as I can remember, I've revered Cher. It's been a loving consumption of mine—some might say idol worship. But I prefer enthusiastic admiration."

My husband shook his head and took another swig. The girls were still and looked constipated.

I continued, telling them about how as a kid, I made long nails out of Scotch tape to look like Cher's and colored them using magic markers. I told them about how my Cher doll is hermetically sealed in a safe in my closet. And how upset I got when, two days after I bought her, her shoes went missing. I think my brother swallowed them just to spite me. And when I saw her signature on one of her album covers, I copied it, pretending to sign autographs as her.

By the time I concluded, my husband was drunk. The girls raised their eyebrows and smiled. "Wow," was all they said. They didn't entirely get it—or me—but they never held it against me, either. And to their credit, they were supportive, with an appropriate amount of caution.

One day, my husband called me at work to tell me he was playing cards at Amy and Kelly's apartment in Reseda. If I wanted to, I should come over. I don't play cards, but I wasn't passing up a potential opportunity to learn something about Cher's personal life, Chastity's, or both. I'd like to state for the record that I wouldn't have done anything with the information. That, too, would be hermetically sealed. It was enough to know something about the woman who had been such a positive and inspiring influence in my life. And I liked the feeling of being on the inside—like I'm part of the crew. Macramé-ing friendship bracelets was right around the corner. I'd agreed to let my husband and the girls set up a drum circle in my kitchen and a horn section in my bathtub. Since I was going along with the disruption and inconvenience like a good team player, I thought it was only fair that the girls share the wealth. Scheduling a playdate with her highness was the least they could do.

The card game was in full swing when I arrived at the girls' apartment. After quick hellos, I walked into the kitchen and grabbed a slice of pizza from the box on the counter. When I lowered the lid, Chastity Bono stood before me. I froze. *What?! How? Why?*

Her hair was darker than when she'd appeared on her parents' television show in the 1970s. A shoulder-length, bilevel haircut had replaced her blonde pigtails—pigtails that I too wore back in the day. We had so much in common. She wore jeans, a nondescript gray T-shirt, and black Doc Martens. I may have blacked out for a few seconds.

"Dani, this is Chas. Chas, Dani," Kelly yelled without looking up from her cards. *No shit! Like Chastity needs a goddamn introduction.*

"Hi, Dani, nice to meet you."

Did she just say my name?

I blinked rapidly, trying to come to. I was sure I was dreaming.

I didn't want Chastity to think I knew (or cared) about her family tree. So I avoided eye contact and mumbled an easy, "Hey." It bordered on assholery. I wasn't starstruck, honestly—I was just struck dumb. When I woke up that morning, I didn't expect my childhood to greet me over a greasy pizza.

When I was a kid, Sunday nights meant sitting in front of the TV watching *The Sonny and Cher Comedy Hour*. I was hypnotized every time Cher put her unique spin on the groovy pop songs of the day with sparkly theatrical flair. The comic banter between her and Sonny always made me laugh, and kind of reminded me of how my parents bantered. But the episodes that featured Chastity were my favorite. I thought she was the luckiest kid alive. I suppose I lived vicariously through her. My mom didn't parade around our apartment in Bob Mackie gowns while singing into a slender white microphone. And my dad wasn't the least interested in pratfalling over furniture. I wanted the life I saw on TV—a life filled with crazy costumes, fan kicks, and celebrity guest appearances.

Thankfully, Chastity grabbed something out of the refrigerator and went into the living room to make a phone call. I sat at the makeshift card table and stared at Amy and Kelly, steaming.

"How could you not prepare me after everything I told you?" And then I wondered if they told Chastity about me. They started giggling. I'm sure it was all quite entertaining for them, watching me worm around in my skin. They had zero grasp of the impact meeting Chastity had on me. They couldn't understand how impossible it was to be in her presence.

A few weeks later, I came home from grocery shopping and saw Chastity playing the tambourine in front of a microphone set up in our hallway. I stood by the stove, just out of sight, listening to her aggressively hit the leather surface. My husband and the girls sat behind computers in the guest bedroom, which we'd converted into a music studio. They were rehearsing for an upcoming live show. When they stopped for a bathroom break, my husband found me unpacking groceries.

"Hey, do you want to sing some backup with Chas?"

I dropped the cans of beans on the counter. "I thought you'd never ask. Maracas too?"

He laughed. "Sure."

He was throwing me a bone—even if he didn't understand where I was coming from and why.

I grabbed a maraca from a shelf of instruments and joined Chas in front of the mic stand. We stood shoulder to shoulder, shaking, rattling, and la-la-la-ing. This is what I imagined heaven to be like.

It was undeniable—Chas was a part of my life now. I nearly buckled under the weight of the idea. We oohed and ahhed, our mouths almost touching. She was a laboratory specimen, and I inspected the pores on her face and the hairs on her head. My thoughts drowned out the music. *Cher probably kissed those pores and touched that piece of hair. Her flesh and blood is swaying on my white shag rug.* I was about to pull the blue punk Cher wig from my closet, put it on, and ask Chas, in my best Cher impression, "Do I remind you of anyone?" But fortunately, Kelly yelled, "Cut," and the music stopped, as did my impulse.

I went outside onto the porch to catch my breath. Not two minutes later, Chas sat down next to me. She started talking about her dad's funeral months earlier as if I had been in the church with her family and friends. I didn't have the heart to tell her that I wasn't there sitting in a pew but had watched the service on television at home, crying. Maybe I should've felt flattered that she was comfortable around me, but it made me self-conscious. I'd watched her and her mother sing on *The Cher Show* in matching orange jumpsuits. And now, she was baring her soul while smoking cigarettes on my porch, looking out at the Mitzvah Store. Was this my new reality now? I didn't know what to say. Never in all my Cher-related fantasies had this conversation ever come up. And then I couldn't stop thinking about the most insensitive things I could say—which happens when I'm nervous or uncomfortable. *"Did you sing in the car with your dad when he drove you to school?"*

"Okay, we're ready," my husband yelled out the window, saving me from myself.

A couple of days later, Amy and Kelly were at our apartment. I passed the guest bedroom/recording studio in between songs and stopped in the doorway. The girls told my husband they'd been at Cher's house in Malibu over the weekend. Their nonchalance was unconscionable.

"So, what did you guys do?" I asked, because I'm a masochist.

"We played board games," Amy said.

Her words felt like tiny paper cuts dipped in hot sauce.

"I love games!" I screamed. "Take me home!"

The girls chuckled, but I wasn't laughing. Why wasn't anyone taking me seriously?

"I mean it."

"We can bring her the next time, can't we?" Kelly asked Amy. I wanted to wrap my arms around Kelly because she went to bat for me.

"I promise," Amy said, "it'll happen."

After dishing about that initial weekend sleepover, every now and again, Amy would call late on a Friday afternoon to ask if we could pick up their dog, Buster, at their apartment and dog sit for the evening. They were at Cher's house and wanted to spend the night, but they hadn't made plans for Buster. I was tired of imagining what their sleepovers were like. I wanted to pack my toothbrush and tongue scraper and see for myself. Did Cher make coffee in the morning? Did she allow shoes in the house? What did her front doorbell sound like?

"I know, I know. I'm sorry for the last-minute call," Amy pleaded. And then Kelly would chime in and promise it wouldn't happen again.

But we all knew that it would.

There were limits to my generosity. My well of kindness was drying up. Why couldn't the girls plan ahead? *Why should I babysit your dog while you play games with Cher?*

The girls stopped by our apartment on their way home after one of their Malibu Cher weekends. "Close your eyes and hold out your hands," Kelly instructed me. Something metal fell into my palms.

"Okay, open your eyes."

I looked down at several long rusty nails.

"It's from the construction site at Cher's new house," Kelly squealed. After several delays, Cher had finally broken ground on what would become her Italian villa high on a bluff overlooking the Pacific Ocean.

"This is hysterical," I cheered. "Thank you!"

"Wait," Kelly said, "there's more." She handed me six scraps of paper. Each one had Cher's signature on it. They looked exactly like the ones I'd signed on my social studies book cover. "They're from the board game."

I would've preferred a sock or a feather boa. I would've even settled for an oven mitt. But I didn't dare complain.

"It'll happen—you'll see." Kelly's tone was self-assured, and I believed her.

"Yeah, it's just timing," Amy whispered sweetly.

I accepted the girls' offerings with grace. At least I was in their thoughts. Even though they were guilt-ridden thoughts. By the way,

I could have sold Cher's autographs to the highest bidder on the internet or the black market. But I gave Amy and Kelly my word that I wouldn't. Instead, I laminated them. They're in the safe with the Cher doll.

The empty promises and the stolen gifts were like carrots dangled in front of my nose. The girls continued to string me along for years, and I kept the faith. But I wasn't any closer to meeting Cher.

After a while, Chas's presence in my apartment barely registered. And the idea of gaining membership to Club Cher withered. My relationships with the girls and Chas normalized. I don't mean to sound jaded, but the shiny new object dulled.

Then, in 2000, I went with Amy, Kelly, and Chas to Cher's *Believe* concert at the Staples Center. Days before, there were rumblings about backstage passes and post-concert bubbly. The concert reignited my hopes for an introduction. I also wanted a plan and a written guarantee, but I kept my mouth shut. At this point, I was outwardly indifferent. Attending the show with Chas was already weird and remarkable. But deep down, I wanted to be ushered backstage by big, burly security guards with lanyards hanging from their necks (and from mine), through dark tunnels and up spiral staircases.

I'd waited decades for this moment.

I also wrestled with how I'd feel if my childhood daydreams and admiration for this woman turned out to be a colossal disappointment. What if my expectations were unrealistic? I argued it was better to meet her now as an adult than if I were still that impressionable, idealistic, and gullible child. I was no longer that seven-year-old little girl who wished she'd been adopted so she might one day find out that Cher was her biological mom. I was over that. Now, it was more like we were professional colleagues. And I set my sights on opening for her on her next tour.

The concert was an incredible spectacle—in the most fantastic way. I danced for two hours straight, singing every word to every song at full volume, much to the ire and eye-rolling of the people sitting directly behind me. When the curtain came down, I felt lightheaded, drunk on nostalgia. I looked toward Chas, who was on her cell phone. No doubt she was talking to her mom, confirming the location of her dressing room. My body was tingling.

Game time.

"Sorry," Chas said, looking into my eyes. "My mom went straight home," and shoved her phone into her back pocket.

"It's fine," I fake laughed. Inside, I was heartbroken.

On the drive home, Chas remarked that watching me watch her mom was more entertaining than watching her mom. Did her comment soothe my broken heart? A little. I also wondered if the girls had called a secret meeting with Chas, and they'd decided I wouldn't come within ten feet of Cher for her own safety.

Listening to Chas talk to her mom, asking her if we could come backstage, sounded like any kid's request of a parent—"Can my friends come over tonight?" And Cher's probable, "Not tonight, honey, I'm pooped," was a typical response from any ordinary working parent. It put things in a different perspective for me. Cher wasn't the celebrity I'd put on a pedestal when I was a kid. She was an exhausted mom at the end of a long week who undoubtedly looked forward to putting on a pair of sweatpants while an assistant rubbed her hammer toe and massaged her scalp and eyelids.

On a Friday night not long after the concert, my husband met me and our dog, Little Ricky, at the back door of our apartment. He was holding the cordless phone out toward me. "It's for you."

"Who is it?" I snapped. I hadn't noticed a rip in the doodie bag until it was too late. "I touched Little Ricky's shit. Can you please tell whoever it is I'll call them back?"

Ignoring my request, my husband followed me into the bathroom.

"What are you doing?" I asked while I scrubbed my hands raw.

"You have to take the call now," he said, grinning.

I grumbled while drying my hands and then took the phone. "Hello?"

"Hi, this is Cher."

"Who?" I repeated. I could barely hear the mellow voice on the other end.

"Cher."

"Who?"

"Cher."

I made Cher repeat herself—twice. My face flushed, and I looked over at my husband, who was quietly laughing.

"I'm going to kill her," I said matter-of-factly.

Cher laughed that recognizable throaty laugh. "Who, Amy?"

"Yes."

I cast Cher as my good pal. It was a reflex. I acted like I'd seen her the day before at Safeway, where we made fun of our mutual friend Amy while we picked out gum and mints.

"Congratulations on your star on the Hollywood Walk of Fame," I said. Two weeks earlier, Sonny and Cher had received a star. I hoped that bringing it up would impress her and keep her talking.

"Yeah, that was cool." She sounded so relaxed. I imagined her lounging by a kidney-shaped pool in a sequined cowboy hat and ass-less chaps.

"I wish I'd been there," I said as if I'd been invited but couldn't make it because of a dentist appointment. "I really liked *Sonny & Me: Cher Remembers*." The retrospective of Cher's life and career with Sonny had aired the night before. Mentioning her dead ex-husband was a risky move. But my mouth was flapping faster than the neurons were firing.

"Thanks, I think it came out pretty well."

After a brief pause, Cher asked, "Would you mind getting Buster so the girls can stay over?"

And there it was. Amy and Kelly had pimped Cher out to do their bidding.

"Ugh, how hard is it to plan?" I asked, genuinely pissed.

"Is that so?" Cher said with a chortle.

"Maybe it's the fucked-up diet they're on." The girls and my husband had recently started some diet that denies your body food! It made everyone irritable and forgetful.

Cher laughed again. I wish I could've recorded the conversation and bottled her laugh.

What was left to talk about after I agreed to pick up Buster? I didn't want the conversation to get awkward. It really couldn't have gone any better. In many ways, it was the perfect Dani–Cher phone call—casual and fucking surreal!

"It was nice talking to you, Cher," I said, releasing her back to her kidney-shaped pool.

She handed the phone to Amy, who apologized for ambushing me, adding, "Cher was smiling the whole time. So, you'll get Buster?"

I hung up and turned to my husband. "I'm definitely getting invited to game night now."

On the drive to the girls' apartment, I thought about seeing

Cher's actual hair at our sleepover. We'll play charades in our pajamas and kibitz until the wee hours of the morning.

"This one time," I'll tell Cher, "my mom was shopping on Madison Avenue in New York and saw you walking down the street and waved."

Cher smiles. "I remember."

"My mom said she stopped you to say hello.

"If memory serves, she asked for an autograph." Cher giggles.

"That was for you, wasn't it?"

"Ha. I cannot tell a lie."

We'll laugh while eating popcorn from a large sterling silver bowl, watching *Stuck on You* in her home movie theater.

My imaginings nearly caused me to hit a pedestrian on the corner of Sherman Way and Balboa Boulevard that night as I drove.

When I got to the girls' apartment, I leashed Buster with a new testiness and diminished hope. I knew the slumber party would never happen. I wouldn't peek inside Cher's pantry or bond over Gene Simmons from KISS. She wouldn't tell me about bedding him, and I wouldn't tell her that KISS was the first rock concert that I went to when I was twelve and how loud I thought it was. I convinced myself that not rendezvousing was probably for the best. Maybe it was a sign of maturity because I quickly let my disappointment go.

———

Several years later, after my husband became my ex-husband, I emailed Amy and Kelly. I asked them if they would ask Cher for a blurb for the book I'd written and was about to publish. I thought it would be fun. To prevent any misunderstandings, I added, "I'm not interested in tools, autographs, or feathers from a boa." I signed off with, "You owe me."

I wasn't the same person as the one who'd gotten suckered into dog-sitting. My request wasn't about childhood adulation or fanatic fandom. I was an author with a legitimate ask. It'd been a long while since I'd needed Cher to show me what was possible. And now an invitation to game night at her house held little appeal for me—nothing personal, Cher. And even though I hoped the girls would see what a blurb could potentially mean for book sales, I also had enough lived experience not to get my hopes up—again.

I received a text back a couple of days later. "That was funny. We'll see what we can do."

I think we all knew it would never happen. But I had to try. I'm nothing if not a trier.

five

How Much for an Iron Lung?

AFTER FIVE EXCRUCIATING YEARS of living like a monk, my memoir, *The Girlfriend Mom*, was about to be published. I never set out to write a book. But writing had been a way for me to process my breakup with Julian, navigate my relationship with Nicole and Tyler, and try to make sense of it all.

Sitting at my desk in my apartment in Hell's Kitchen, finalizing the dates for my book tour, I was excited to rejoin society. And, with any luck, I'd meet my future second ex-husband on my book tour. It'd been a long, dry spell, and I'd only recently welcomed the idea of dating again. At the very least, I'd press some flesh. The stars seemed to be aligning in my favor.

Fuck you, COVID-19!

Warning. The following story contains disturbing content and may be triggering. Reader discretion is advised.

The virus lurked everywhere. It floated outside my apartment building, traveling freely and undetected in the hallways. My heart raced if I stood by the drafty front door because I was convinced that virus particles were wafting inside. I held my breath under my KN95 mask as I sprinted back and forth to the trash room. I stopped doing laundry in the shared washers and dryers. My neighbor's boxer shorts were definitely saturated with virus spores.

I wondered if Irving and Noreen were hunkered down at the other end of the hall. *What is everyone doing about food?* I was running low on bananas. Walking to the corner market felt like a death march. The elevator buttons were COVID-coated, and the old man walking his schnauzer across the street that I was spying on with my binoculars petrified me. I was shocked and awed by the intensity and swiftness of my paralyzing fear and panic. I didn't know I had it in me. Or maybe it was always in me and it was just napping.

Still, I believed those in charge would have the emergency wrapped up by the time I hit the road and welcomed my fans at bookstores. This would be the big payoff I'd been waiting for. But when the medical community declared a pandemic and implemented a lockdown, any hope of signing books or going out on a date came to a screeching halt.

I spent two hours feeling sorry for myself—all the canceled plans and having to put "my shot" on hold. I whined and shouted at the CDC officials on the evening news. "Why do you hate me?" And then when I saw the makeshift morgues set up in my neighborhood, I quickly shut my pie hole. No one's going to accuse me of being self-centered and insensitive.

Instead of buying plane tickets to California, I stocked up on latex gloves, masks, plastic face shields, Vicks VapoRub, Tylenol, Epsom salts, a thermometer, an oxygen meter, and disposable shoe covers. Funnily enough, toilet paper wasn't on my list. I could wing it in a pinch and use a washcloth if I had to. People weren't using their imaginations. Surely, my daily ginger shots and hair and nail vitamins would keep a COVID infection away.

Who knew there were so many varieties of gas masks? I comparison shopped and bookmarked my favorites. If, for some reason, I couldn't get out of my apartment on the thirty-ninth floor through the front door, I thought about an alternate escape route. A friend recommended I buy a rope ladder to climb down to the rooftop on the thirty-second floor and then take it from there. But first, I'd have to figure out how to unlock the child-proof window so it opened more than just a few inches. Or I could buy a wingsuit, squeeze through the crack, and paraglide down to street level like a flying squirrel. I bookmarked those product pages as well.

I'd read somewhere that blowing up balloons keeps the lungs clear and strong. As a Pilates instructor, to me the idea made a certain kind of sense. Breathing uses the diaphragm—the primary muscle below the lungs. If that was strong, then the lungs above could easily ward off intruders. I bought a small variety pack, not realizing until after the fact that if I didn't tie the end, I really only needed one. After ten minutes of inflating and deflating, I was bored and I had a pounding headache. I stared at the bag of balloons. *What a waste.*

I went on YouTube and searched for a tutorial on making balloon animals. Unfortunately, the balloons I'd bought were too small. You need the long ones to make anything bigger than a turd. Undeterred, I pulled out my bike pump, inflated the bag of balloons, knotted them, and bam! Party decorations.

"Oh, I never touch elevator buttons, public handles, or escalator railings, even when there isn't a pandemic," I bragged in those early days. "I'm a writer. I already live like a hermit. It's not a stretch." I wore my pronouncement like the Presidential Medal of Freedom. It gave me the illusion that the horror "out there" was just an average Tuesday and nothing to worry about.

My publicist had set up phone interviews and promotional appearances on Zoom. They were all firsts for me. I was looking forward to them, but I was also nervous. I had no idea how I'd come across meeting people on my computer screen set up in my bedroom. I always thought I appeared friendlier and funnier in person—especially if my intended audience had been drinking.

At the same time, I also felt a profound sense of injustice and anger toward anyone who couldn't and wouldn't do the right thing—according to me and the National Institutes of Health. Walking in New York became an Olympic sport—and highly competitive. I moved in and out of lanes on the Hudson River Greenway like a human car, weaving around joggers, electric bicycles, and scooters. Everyone was a potential COVID spike protein carrying a load of contagion. If I spotted someone coughing or sneezing, I picked up my pace. My fellow Olympians often strayed from the recommended six feet of social distance, so I'd walk with my arms outstretched in a T position, like Jesus on his cross, to provide them with visual spacing.

As I walked, I listened to music on my headphones and sang out loud. I'd decided that singing also helped lung capacity. Whenever I passed someone infringing on my personal space, I yelled, "Move the fuck over!" This got less of a reaction than you might think. Most New Yorkers talk to themselves in public anyway, and no one bats an eye, so as far as anyone knew, I could've been yelling at myself. But my shouts were very pointed. I wanted to tattle on anyone not following the rules and scream, "Don't be a dick."

It should come as no surprise that my favorite job in elementary school was hall monitor.

One awful morning, I found myself waiting in line at the urgent care up the street. My head was throbbing, and I was unusually tired. When it was my turn, I sat on the examining table looking straight ahead (as recommended) while addressing the nurse standing to my right.

"Thank you for your service." I thought I might cry.

"You're welcome." And then she tickled my brain with a cotton swab. "You'll have the results in a few days."

Quarantining in my apartment only increased my anxiety. *What if my oxygen levels drop? If I bang on a neighbor's door, will they be too frightened to answer?* This is one of only a truckload of negatives to living alone. I supposed dialing 911 was an option, but it had to be an extreme emergency. As kids, my brother and I were conditioned to believe that a broken bone, vomiting a kidney, or shitting an intestine wasn't cause for alarm. According to my dad, "You're fine unless you're bleeding."

During this time of the pandemic, my parents, who were in their late seventies, were hunkered down in Florida, where they lived for half the year. Who knew when they'd be able to return to New York. As far as I was concerned, they were sitting ducks. In addition to their age, their other vulnerabilities made them susceptible to COVID—my dad's heart condition and hearing loss, and my mom's extensive periodontal needs and her swervy driving.

In the last few years, watching them get older has been sobering—more so for them, I imagine. Whenever the idea of mortality comes up, specifically theirs, I shriek, "What are you talking about? You're never going to die." I can't tell the truth in front of them because it makes it too real, and I'm immature.

Their impending demise brought up worries and questions. Do I know where they keep their passwords to their bank accounts and life insurance policies? Who gets stuck with my mom's collection of measuring cups, tongs, and watering cans, me or my brother? And I don't want to go to Florida and retrieve their bodies. But if COVID took them, I was confident nothing had been left unsaid between us. My parents knew where they'd failed me, and I'd apologized for my expensive wedding mistake on a seventeenth-century Dutch farm that smelled of cow manure and regret.

My parents have been at each other's side for over sixty years. Most days, they're attached to each other at their original hips. It'd be so romantic if they checked out together—much too devastating for the parent left behind if they don't. Maybe they'd slip into a peaceful coma while watching and reading the closed captions of some Turkish series like *Kulüp* that they're so fond of. My dad in his favorite club chair with the ass indentation so severe it ensures no other ass will ever be comfortable sitting in it. My mom curled up on the couch beside him, her sticky fingers limp in a Costco-size bag of popcorn. I can't imagine planning two separate Shivas if they don't go together.

Something shifted between us when my parents and I spoke after we went into lockdown. Somehow, our roles were blurring. We were relating to one another more like equals and not within the parent-child dynamic that I understood. I didn't like it. I wanted their reassurance that everything would be okay. Wasn't that their job as parents? Soothing words in times of grave devastation. "It'll

be fine. We won't die. And we won't let you die either. Trust us."
But the words never came, because they didn't know if it would be
okay—no one did—and they couldn't fake it.

My parents were never traditional in their parenting. They
brought little discipline and were too permissive for my taste. But
now, behaving more like friends and equals didn't work for me either.
I never understood kids calling a parent their friend or their hero.
C'mon. COVID brought out the true heroes. Okay, fine. If your
mom or dad ran into a burning building to save you and your Playbill
collection (for example), they might qualify as heroes. Otherwise, no.
I remember one time when I called my mom my hero.

My dad threw my mom a fiftieth birthday party in the backyard
of their house. He'd hired a DJ, set up a tent, and had an open bar.
When the DJ played Bette Midler's "Wind Beneath My Wings," I
reflexively grabbed my mom and pulled her on to the dance floor.
I loved the song and thought it would make her feel special if I
serenaded her. I stared into her eyes, sang with Bette, and yelled in
her face about flying high like an eagle, standing in my shadow, and
being my hero.

It was the final scene in the schmaltzy Hallmark movie in my
head. At last, my mom admits to her gambling addiction. She apol-
ogizes for losing my college tuition money at the roulette wheel and
pleads for my forgiveness. She's been going to meetings and promises that *this* time will be different. This dance is our second chance.
The song crescendos, the scene ends, and the credits roll.

When I snapped out of my hallucination, I was swaying with
my mom and became self-conscious. Everyone was staring at us and
most likely thinking, *What the hell is she doing now?* Meanwhile, my
mom isn't my hero or the wind beneath my wings. I was acting!

I decided to drive to my parents' house in the suburbs north of Manhattan, where I could hop off Jesus's cross and walk with my arms at my sides. I felt a little guilty for abandoning my neighbors, but then I remembered the maskless Covidiots on the bike path failing to meet my standards and expectations. Staying at the house meant no one else would be around, and I'd have enough space to pace on grass instead of dog-shit-stained pavement. I had to protect my sanity and my life. I pushed past my headache, got in the car, and set out.

With Manhattan in my rearview mirror, I pulled into my parents' driveway. A dirty brown pickup truck was parked in front of the garage. Tools and ladders spilled out of the cargo bed. A man and a woman in their late fifties, both wearing coveralls and work boots, leaned casually against the truck.

"What are you doing here?" I mouthed through my closed car window.

"We're fixing the broken fence," the woman answered, maskless and lighting a cigarette.

When I told my mom I was staying at the house while waiting for my test results, she said workers would be coming to fix the fence. If there's a home repair or improvement on my mom's to-do list, not even a pandemic is stopping that shit from happening. The woman was blowing COVID through her smoke rings. I stayed in the car and cracked my window just enough for my voice to escape.

"We're going to start working if that's okay," the woman said.

"I guess. Shouldn't you guys be wearing masks?"

The woman stared at me. "Well, we're outside, and you're in the car, so . . ."

Inside the house, I locked the door behind me and cried out, "I made it."

I dropped my suitcase in the hallway and walked into the kitchen. As soon as I set up my laptop on the counter, my phone rang. It was my mom on FaceTime. I answered the call on my computer.

"Hi."

"How are you feeling?" my mom asked.

"I'm okay."

My cell phone rang. "Hi, Dad."

"Are you on the phone with Mom?" he asked.

"Well, technically, she's on my laptop. Staring right at her. Why?"

"Can she hear me?" His tone was cagey, and I imagined him twirling the hairs at the ends of his mustache.

"Do you want her to hear you?"

"Yes," he answered. "Can you put me on speaker so I can hear her?"

I did and then sat by as they routed their conversation through my phone, to my laptop, back to each other.

"We can drop the mirror off at Barry's frame store when we get back to New York," my dad suggested to my mom.

"Let's leave it for now," she said. "I'm not sure where I want it."

The conversation devolved into when they thought Barry might retire from the framing business—he was seventy-five. And then my dad hung up. No "goodbye" or "see you later." He does this occasionally, on the phone, or he'll walk away in the middle of a conversation without warning. I used to think it was his hearing loss, but now I just think he's rude.

After I unpacked my suitcase, I set up a workspace in the den. I had several Zoom interviews coming up that I had to prepare for. Promoting the book was a welcomed distraction. But it also felt trivial in the face of possible death. The test results were still several days away, and I was on the edge. The waiting was hell. But as long as I wasn't experiencing any debilitating symptoms, I was determined not to let COVID spoil my book launch.

The first Zoom interview was with an editor from a local newspaper. "Do you think the definition of family has shifted over the years?" she asked.

"Yes. There isn't a one-size-fits-all," I answered. "Just as there are a million unique ways a woman can be a mom, the same is true for a woman who chooses not to be a mom." A million unique ways? Ugh. My nerves took over. I wouldn't let the interviewer speak. I was a runaway train. It was like I only had one minute left to live and had to share every thought I ever had about anything and everything.

In the afternoon, I dawdled around the house like I was on a school field trip to Hyde Park. I had no personal attachments to this house because it wasn't the one I grew up in. I don't have any memories of it independent of my parents. I stopped in my dad's library and pulled *Life* by Keith Richards from one of the shelves. When I opened the cover, several pieces of frail, yellowed paper fell on the floor. I shook my head and smiled. Crack open any book of my dad's and you'll find hastily folded newspaper clippings behind the front cover or squished between pages—a related article or an interview with the author. It was hard enough getting through books like *Crime and Punishment* (per his suggestion) when I was in school. But then he'd leave supporting materials on my bed, in case I thirsted for more after reading 720 pages. My dad is nothing if not thorough—and a bit of a show-off.

It's always been my belief that if a house has two or more bedrooms, an attic, and a basement, it's a slasher movie set. I was a ball of tension sleeping that first night, even with the security alarm on. I'd lived in the city for so long that I'd forgotten about the sights and sounds of nature. The rustling wind, crackling tree branches, and what sounded like marbles rolling in the attic made for a restless sleep. I assumed the marbles rolling were animals on the roof, not hungry children trying to get my attention. The unidentified noises only added to the stress of my health concerns.

My house fears date back to when we moved into one from our apartment—apartments where nothing terrible or scary ever happened. The only noises I heard came from us kids screaming while running up and down the hallways. In the new house, I constantly imagined the worst. I had a mental checklist I'd go through every night before falling asleep in the event of a home invasion. Where would I hide? Where was the closest phone? Where were my glasses so I could see the phone? I'd practice holding my breath in case I ever had to crouch in the closet until the intruder moved on to my brother's room next door. All those years practicing my death scene would come in handy if I couldn't make it to the closet. My lifeless body under my blanket would assure the intruder that there were no eyewitnesses.

In the morning, I made coffee and called my mom. "Can I walk around downstairs if the alarm is on?"

"I don't know." Her lack of knowledge grated on my last nerve. My tolerance for any manner of uncertainty was dwindling.

"After fifteen years, how can you not know?" Based on her silence, she was either playing Words with Friends or ordering something she already had two of from the Apple store.

"Put the code in and press 'stay,'" my mom said. "It should be okay."

"Should be? Never mind."

I heard a noise coming from the dining room.

"Mom, something sounds like tiny pebbles hitting a window."

"Where's it coming from?"

"The dining room," I said.

"Sometimes small birds try to get in through the window."

"But the windows are shut."

"Right," she said, "it's their tiny heads ramming into the glass."

Cold, hard facts.

"That's awful."

"They'll tire themselves out eventually."

"I gotta go, Mom."

I stood in the dining room and watched as two small birds flew at top speed into the window and then ricocheted off. They backed up and took another run. I admired their perseverance. But I couldn't bear to witness such cruelty and stupidity. I googled "how to stop birds from committing suicide."

Hour by hour, the news about the pandemic continued to get worse. I was grateful for the minutiae task of choosing a font for my book's chapter titles. What was sure to have been a turning point in my career became a joyless and pointless exercise. Still, what else was there to do? And I hadn't come this far to stop just short of the finish line. I tried focusing on the positives. Glowing reviews. High praise from strangers. Breathing.

During the endless wait, I'd learned to craft DIY face masks from old yarmulkes I found in my parents' Passover closet. I watched a few YouTube videos and Martha Stewarted the hell out of those satin kippot. I did some light gardening and watered the houseplants. I played plumber and replaced some cracked toilet seat covers with slow-close lids. Humble brag. I decalcified the washing

machine and dishwasher and ensured the lint trap wasn't a fire haz-
ard. What I didn't do was bake bread. Why would I? So I could die
with a belly resembling a sourdough loaf?

Speaking of food, after two days I'd eaten everything from
the refrigerator that didn't require cooking and had moved on to
the freezer.

"What is this?" I asked my mom on a FaceTime call. I tapped a
bag of unidentified frozen meat on the counter. "Do you think it's
safe to eat?" I was asking the wrong person. According to my mom,
all food can be bagged, sealed, and frozen with an expiration date
of never.

My mom squinted. "It looks like chicken breasts. Where did
you find it?"

"It's a block of ice. Where do you think I found it? Bye, Mom."

At 4:30 a.m., on day three, the house alarm went off, startling
me from a deep sleep. I grabbed my glasses, jumped off the bed,
and ran into my parents' bedroom. I entered the code on the alarm
panel. Three seconds later, the alarm company called. I picked up
the cordless house phone.

"Is everything okay?" the voice on the other end asked.

"Yeah. I don't know what happened. Maybe it was the wind."
I had no evidence of this. But I also didn't want to entertain any
other explanation.

"Can you tell me the password?" the operator asked.

I stalled. There were two options. I tossed one out.

"Yes, thank you," he said. "Do you need us to send someone over?"

"No, it's okay." I didn't know if it was okay.

If I wanted any chance of going back to sleep, I had to do a thorough sweep of the interior. I pulled on the white fleece shirt I'd found

in a drawer days earlier, dropped the phone into the breast pocket, and padded downstairs. I searched every room except the basement—nothing good ever comes from a basement in the middle of the night.

A strong breeze blew into the kitchen from the family room. I walked that way. The French doors to the patio were wide open, as if someone had just walked out—or in. A full moon backlit the furniture. Coming off of the tripped alarm, it was a little too dramatic and ominous for my taste. I decided that the wind must've blown the doors open. I remembered having trouble locking them earlier in the day after going into the backyard.

There was something wrong with the lock, and I couldn't secure it. So I pushed an ottoman up against the doors. But when I stepped back, I wasn't convinced it would hold. I grabbed a stool from the kitchen and set it on top of the ottoman. I still didn't think it was heavy enough. I went into the laundry room and found the skinniest upright vacuum you've ever seen. I slid it behind the French door handles. It reminded me of the scene in *The Graduate* when Dustin Hoffman locks the people in the church with the enormous cross.

Just when my head hit the pillow, headlights from a car in the driveway lit up my bedroom. I held my breath, just like I'd practiced, but stopped short of hiding in the closet. Instead, I knelt on the bed and peeked through the slats of the blinds. *Maybe this is a home invasion after all. Is that the getaway car? I don't want to die!* After some tense moments, a figure emerged from the driver's seat carrying a flashlight. It was a policeman. I'd told Alarm Man I didn't need help. Why doesn't anyone listen to me?

I flew downstairs just as the officer's beam of light moved from the front of the house around to the back. He stopped on the patio.

I saw his head tilting from side to side. I imagined him radioing to his superiors, "By the looks of things, whoever's inside might be in serious danger. I may need backup." I approached the French doors and began explaining.

The officer cut me off. "Can we meet around the front?" he shouted over the wind. "I have some questions." I bet you do.

I sprinted up the stairs to my bedroom and made a costume change. I swapped out the four-sizes-too-large-for-me fleece for a cute tan duster. You only get one chance to make a first impression. And how many first impressions did I have left? It was five in the morning, and I could've been on the precipice of COVID—and death.

I opened the front door. The officer was young and cute. And I was glad I'd changed clothes. He asked me for my name, address, phone number, and birthdate.

"Birthdate? Why?" I smiled. "Are you going to send me a birthday present?"

He laughed.

"That ottoman vacuum Macgyvered thingy probably looked suspect, huh?"

"Yeah, it looks weird—I've never seen that before."

It was my turn to laugh.

"So, same time tomorrow?" I wanted to ask. I wanted to tell him that I might have COVID and could be six feet under by noon, so if he was game, maybe one for the road?

The following afternoon, despite the possibility of finding small children decomposing or playing marbles in a corner, I cleaned out the attic. I needed a project to take my mind off of everything and give my hands something to do. It was a preemptive strike—a jump start on all the affairs that would need tending to after my parents' inevitable demise, whether from COVID or old age. I thought I'd mitigate the trauma of having to touch their belongings after they're gone. I don't want to sift through their past while grieving and inconsolable. I'll be too busy writing the eulogy. I know me.

Decluttering when my parents were alive also meant that I could get their input while avoiding my actual motivation for the clean-out. I wouldn't have to be responsible for deciding what stayed and what got tossed. I was doing them a favor. They weren't about to get down on their knees and sort through water-stained boxes and mildewy rug scraps themselves.

The Norelco hair dryer from the '60s sat in the middle of the attic. It was the color of cement with mustard yellow trim. It was advertised as a professional home dryer, the same as the ones they used in beauty parlors. When I was little, on special occasions, my mom would set my hair in big fat wire rollers after I took a bath. I think the bath was the special occasion. She'd lift the space helmet dome, I'd crawl underneath, and then she'd lower it above my head. My mom would unroll my hair when it was dry, leaving it smooth and bouncing on my shoulders. I felt as glamorous as a movie star. There were too many memories to throw out the dryer, so I set it off to the side.

I looked around. There was so much material chaos, which only added to my mental chaos. Three busted laundry baskets lay lifeless beside several corroded and torn window screens. I counted eight suitcases, all missing one or more wheels. Why were these being saved? My mom had Christmas decorations and wrapping paper stored away in a tall plastic container. For what? The last time we celebrated Christmas, Monica Lewinsky was *just* an incoming White House intern.

My parents and I are so different. Where they believe more is more and any available space should be covered or filled, I prefer taking up space with my personality, not with material possessions. My mom's old artist's portfolio leaned against a half wall covered in cobwebs. It was odd that she'd keep her artwork stashed away and not framed and displayed around the house. One by one, I gently thumbed through the delicate papers: a stencil of well-worn cowboy boots, a sketch of the brass-and-wood dinner bell from my childhood. (My mom rang that bell every night like she was the cook on a cattle drive in the Wild West—"Dinner! Come and git it.") And then I paused on the last drawing, a charcoal portrait of a naked man with a bushy mustache. *Dad?!* It took me a moment to consider my mom's crude rendering of my dad's nude body. And crude it was—abstract art, really.

Wow, that was unexpected. So randy. So experimental. It made me question, how well did I know these people? I felt like I was riffling through some stranger's intimate inner life. I put the portfolio back where I found it.

In the back corner of the room, boxes of slide carousels were stacked on top of one another, like ghosts were in the middle of a game of Jenga. Slideshows were popular during family gatherings in our house. My dad would take the screen and the slide projector from the hall closet and set them up in the living room. My mom would pick one or two carousels. We never knew what we would see because the slides weren't always chronological. A few boudoir shots of our cat, Cindy, might be followed by a photo montage of my brother and me standing outside a liquor store in Tijuana, Mexico, while our parents waited in line to buy bottles of Kahlúa. I wanted to digitize the slides once it was safe to be in stores again. Thousands of images on a thumb drive would make it super easy to create a slideshow for my parents' memorial service.

Near the slides, a crushed Rubbermaid storage bin sat beside a reel-to-reel film projector. I wondered why my parents hadn't entrusted it to me instead of letting it rust and languish up here in obscurity. I had attended two film schools, after all. I opened the bin. Silver metal canisters of 8 mm film spilled out of a ripped shopping bag. Red spools of celluloid had unraveled several feet or so. It was a careless way of preserving our home movies, and I rewound the films as best as I could.

I picked up several canisters and read the peeling and cruddy labels written in my dad's chicken scratch. And then I started rocking back and forth. "Two Lesbians—artful." "Bath scene—great ending." "Two guys kissing—very good."

Dad, always with the opinions.

The sheer volume of canisters made me wonder if my parents had run an adult movie theater when my brother and I were away at camp. While my parents were aqua jogging in face shields in the Sunshine State, I was hyperventilating in the attic among their smut.

It might not have been a big deal if my parents and I *were* friends. We might've shared a laugh—perhaps compared movie reviews. But we weren't friends. We have roles. Parents. Children. Boundaries. End of story. I'd never share intimate details of my personal life with them. They don't even know I wear a mouthguard to bed.

What can I say? When I'm eighty and my parents are a hundred and four, I'll likely still think this way. I always wanted clear boundaries and structure. And because my parents were largely ineffectual in this department, I'd often have to be the one to set them, like when I was ten years old and told my parents, "Do not, under any circumstances, ask me business questions that could determine the fate of our family's financial future ever again."

I darted from the attic and tripped over a straw sombrero on my way out.

For some reason, I told my mom what I'd unearthed.

"When you open Pandora's box, you never know what you're gonna find." My mom continued, laughing, "You're a little late. Your brother found those containers decades ago. He said it fell off a shelf in our closet. Please."

Telling her was an unexpected relief, and it was surprising to feel like a burden was lifted. Maybe it was time to loosen the reins and relax a little.

"Dad said to leave everything alone."

"My pleasure."

As I was talking with my mom, my phone pinged with a voice-mail notification. It was from the urgent care clinic. I told her to hang on while I listened to it.

"You tested positive for COVID," an anonymous female voice reported. She continued with instructions, but after "positive," all I heard was, "Get your affairs in order." I wondered how long before my breathing became shallow. *How much does an iron lung cost?* My hysteria felt justified, and not because of my affinity for the theatrical. This was before the vaccines rolled out.

The first thing I did was order groceries for delivery; I didn't want to run out of bananas again. But instead of getting what I'd ordered—eggs, bread, fruits, and vegetables—Instacart mistakenly delivered three bags of rice cakes and a ham. After several calls to the store, I was told, "Due to COVID, we can't take them back. We're very sorry."

I can't eat your sorry!

While I was lying in bed with a fever and a numb ass—a lesser-known side effect of COVID—my book was published. It was out in the world and out of my control—like everything else at the time. There wasn't a celebration marking the event, but I'd gotten back my sense of smell and taste and celebrated with a long overdue shower.

It'd been weeks since I escaped from New York City, and now that I felt like myself again, I wanted to return to my life. My apartment building had put up a plastic barrier around the front desk. I was happy to see precautions being taken. I thought again about my self-prescribed role within the (perhaps) outdated parent-child model. I didn't care about any of it. The only thing I cared about was keeping my parents alive and laughing with them, or at them, for as long as possible. Still, I could never imagine a world where my parents and I watch one of their smutty art films together and discuss character development and lighting.

What I did imagine was a changing world for the better. How could it not be during a pandemic with all that we'd been through? People would be kinder, gentler, and more compassionate. If not now, when? We needed each other. I saw a news story about my fellow New Yorkers donating plastic visors and surgical masks to customers at the local bodega. I felt hopeful and more connected to my neighbors and mail carrier.

While I waited for the elevator in my building one afternoon, a man in his thirties, unmasked, wearing spandex biking shorts (which should be outlawed), rolled in from the service entrance with his bicycle. He wheeled to a stop next to me. Masking and social distancing were still firm suggestions.

"Do you have a mask?" I gently asked.

"I was riding my bike," he answered, looking away.

"Yeah, I can see that, but you're inside now." He waved me off and headed into the open elevator.

"Well, I guess I'll tell the building manager then."

"Go ahead," he shouted. "I'm in apartment 901." And just before the elevator door closed, he gave me the finger.

six

You Can Leave Your Hat On, Mr. Lear

IF YOU'D WATCHED AS MUCH television as I had, you knew there wasn't anyone more influential in the medium than Norman Lear. Like millions of others, my childhood was defined by his shows. They made growing up entertaining and tolerable. I escaped into worlds beyond my own. There weren't any junkyards in my suburban town. When I was eleven and watched *Mary Hartman, Mary Hartman*, I vowed never to live in suburbia when I was older. His shows were enlightening, and they challenged my limited understanding of human beings. I watched episodes about adoption, racism, feminism, interracial couples, and anti-Semitism. I spent more time with Weezy and Mrs. Garrett than with my own family.

But most consequential is that Norman Lear is responsible for my love affair with comedy. I didn't grow up knowing anyone famous or in show business. That world was out of reach and also what I was reaching for.

I decided not to share any of this with Lori, my high school friend who called me one day and invited my then husband and me to a going-away party (she was moving to Boston). I didn't want to frighten her. The party was being hosted by her uncle, Mr. Norman Lear, at his house.

"Terrific," I stuttered into the phone.

Lori rattled off her uncle's address nonchalantly, like it was as common as 1600 Pennsylvania Avenue. She didn't seem to be affected at all by her familial tie to television royalty. What the hell was wrong with her? Did she even watch TV? I, on the other hand, scribbled the address on a blue Post-it note and felt like she'd just given me the nuclear launch codes. Lori didn't *know* know me. She should've asked for a background check and for me to send her some references who could vouch for my character. I was in the comfort and safety of my apartment, and I was already sweating and cramping. *Am I actually going to meet Mr. Norman Lear?*

I was going to Lori's party, where I could be scant inches away from the biggest name in television, thereby making me famous by association. If you don't think that was a big deal, then you don't know me at all.

"See you in a few days," I chirped. I hung up the phone and ran to the bathroom.

My husband was out of town on the night of the party, so I went alone, which was probably for the best. He'd seen me in action. I drove my Honda Accord north on the 405, the blue Post-it note stuck to an air vent. Destination, Brentwood. It's an area in LA with expensive upscale homes, fashionable boutiques, and where the (alleged) O. J. Simpson murders occurred. I continued into a canyon, the Santa Monica Mountains rising above and within spitting distance of the Getty Center Museum.

I drove down a tree-lined street, through an opened gate, and into a circular gravel driveway. I parked on the far side of a stone fountain next to some other cars. The canary yellow house was worthy of an *Architectural Digest* cover. Bay windows lined the entire ground floor. Climbing morning glory hugged the white concrete columns on either side of the driveway. It was all pretty grand, in the way mansions are, but it also somehow felt homey and welcoming. I later found out there was a thirty-five-car garage, which made me wonder if Mr. Lear ran a car dealership as a side hustle. I floated along the path to the front door. No security. No metal detectors. No pat down. And then I remembered Lucy.

My parents had taken my brother and me to California when we were eleven and ten. I insisted on paying a visit to Lucille Ball. My dad bought me a map of the stars' homes from a man sitting under a beach umbrella off Sunset Boulevard. We parked across the street from Lucy's white two-story colonial. I was surprised that it was out in the open on a typical residential street—no gate, tall hedges, or electric fence.

With every step on the brick walkway to the front door, I thought about what would happen when I rang the doorbell and Lucy answered. When she heard how far I'd come, surely she'd invite me in for a game of backgammon (her favorite) while my family waited in the car, per my instructions. I wouldn't let them spoil my special moment.

I pressed the doorbell. A speakeasy peephole slid open and revealed a set of dark brown eyes.

"Can I help you?" the faceless male voice asked.

"Is Lucy home?"

"No, she's not."

"Oh, I came from New York. I was hoping to meet her." In my ten-year-old mind, nobody had ever attempted such an act of fearlessness.

"I'm sorry, but she's not home. Goodbye." And with that, the eyes were gone.

If Lucy didn't want visitors coming up to her door, why didn't she erect a concrete wall or build a moat to keep the likes of me out of her front yard?

But now I was going *inside* Norman Lear's house. Take that, Lucy!

"Hey, welcome," Lori purred, opening the front door. "It's so good to see you."

I gave her a hug. "You too. I can't believe you're leaving paradise for snow and ice."

Lori welcomed me into a modest and charming entryway. I'd expected it to be more showy and ostentatious—perhaps a medieval suit of armor flanked by a pair of Doberman pinschers. I handed Lori the bottle of wine I'd brought.

"Oh, you didn't have to bring anything."

"I wasn't raised by wolves."

We walked into the kitchen where Lori put my fifteen-dollar bottle of Cabernet on the counter. It looked so sad next to the bottles in expensive velvet bags. Caterers in black-and-white uniforms holding trays of tiny foods flitted around us. *What is this catering nonsense?* Lori had told me the party was "casual" and "low-key."

I didn't know any of the people standing around the aircraft-carrier-sized white marble island. Lori introduced me to a few of her relatives and friends. I scanned the room, taking it all in. My mom was sure to interrogate me about the decor. Fifteen copper saucepans dangled from a ceiling rack. By contrast, I have two scratched Calphalon pans shoved in the back of a cabinet. I counted three sinks, a double oven, and a twelve-burner stove. I do love appliances, and Norman Lear's did not disappoint. I noted a toaster oven, hand blender, bread maker, and a white Mr. Coffee machine—to keep him humble, I'm guessing.

After I'd committed the inventory to memory, I was fidgety. Thankfully, a waiter appeared with glasses of wine, and I snatched one off his tray.

Lori sidled up next to me. "Are you going to be okay if I mingle?"

"Of course," I said in between gulps. "I'll be fine."

It was absurd to think I'd actually meet Mr. Lear. I'd worked myself into a nervous lather for nothing. He was merely opening his home to his niece and her friends. He was probably upstairs watching *The Real World*. I laughed, imagining him with nothing better to do than ask guests if they wanted more cheese.

I finished my wine and put the glass down beside some crumpled napkins and half-eaten shrimp on a counter. And when I lifted my head, I caught sight of a figure across the aircraft carrier. A figure that I recognized. *What is Norman Lear doing here?* My unease was about to do me in. I was so uncomfortable I started thinking about the most tasteless questions I could ask Mr. Lear. "Hey, Norm! How much do you make in residuals? Does someone iron your pajamas?"

I bit down on my tongue, smiled, and white-knuckled the back of a stool, trying to steady myself. I was close enough to smell Norman Lear's Old Spice aftershave. It was the same one my dad used when I was a kid. Norman looked kingly with his fisherman's bucket hat—or crown, as it were. The hat was as iconic as the man himself—his trademark.

A few courageous souls engaged Mr. Lear in conversation, and I marveled at their ease. I couldn't feel my toes and stood motionless beside the double oven, watching from just out of earshot. I felt like a Catholic getting an audience with the Pope. Or a Jew breaking bread (without the chitchat) with Moses. If someone had told my child self that one day I'd sip wine out of Norman Lear's goblets, I would've said there was a better chance of me finding out that I was adopted and my biological parents were Lou Ferrigno and Shirley Chisholm.

I was afraid of passing out, so I turned and stared up at the saucepans.

I pretended this was *my* uncle's home, where we played Pictionary and watched silent movies on the weekends. I left the room without thinking about where I was going.

In the center of the main hallway was a large iron (or bronze) pillar. It looked like something sculpted by Rodin. Sections were cut out and filled with miniature figurines. I continued to stroll until I found myself in a stately living room. The exposed beams accentuated the size of the floor-to-ceiling windows. Artwork was everywhere—paintings, drawings, and expensive-looking tchotchkes. I was pretty sure that Hopper's *Nighthawks* hung above the fireplace—the original; no reproductions framed at Michael's hanging on these walls. *Wait, are those King Tut's sandals suspended over the tufted loveseat?*

In the far corner of the room was a hat rack. I giggled. I'd always wondered what Norman Lear was hiding underneath his chapeau. Was there some grim truth underneath that he didn't want the world to see? And then I couldn't stop humming the Joe Cocker song "You Can Leave Your Hat On." I imagined Mr. Lear whipping off his hat and tossing it on one of the hooks at the end of a long day of being legendary.

Most guests were still in the kitchen with Lori, so I had the whole house to myself. I had no idea if it was okay to wander around unsupervised. But since no one stopped me, I moseyed into a library. A random couple was leaning against one of the two rolling ladders, gesturing in a heated argument. I hoped they wouldn't acknowledge my presence. I wasn't in the mood for small talk. Fortunately, they were too engrossed in their squabble to notice me.

A mahogany bookcase with deep imposing shelves covered two entire walls. I moved in for a closer look. I thought I was hallucinating. The scripts for all the television shows Norman Lear had created, written, and produced were casually exposed as if they were take-out menus. Why weren't these treasures in a climate-controlled enclosure protecting them from the elements? Why weren't they safeguarded in a bullet-proof glass case like the *Mona Lisa*? They were irreplaceable Hollywood artifacts—more valuable than gold bars, goddamn it. If I were in charge, I'd put the scripts in the bullion vault at Fort Knox. Why wasn't Mr. Lear treating them as the fragile, priceless gems that they were? Forget friggin' Mona—protect the 133 episodes of *Good Times*.

The squabbling couple didn't appear awed at all. From what I could hear, they were preoccupied with the wine stain on the man's white shirt sleeve. They were oblivious to the holy (and first edition) sitcom scriptures in the room.

I reflexively started davening in front of the bookshelf. And then I reached out to touch one of the spines. I hoped a brush against greatness would infuse my anemic job situation with some lofty juju. My career was on life support—running on fumes, really. I was contemplating quitting my job as a personal assistant to a former *SNL* actress. I'd spent too many hours stapling her headshot to her resume. Stapling my face to the fax machine would've been less painful.

My outstretched hand was about to land when I felt someone's hot breath on my neck. I sniffed. *I know that smell.* My body shook, and my face flushed. I turned slowly and guiltily.

Busted.

It was Mr. Lear.

He'd snuck up behind me. I had no idea how much of my attempt to fondle his work he saw, but I braced myself for a reprimand, nevertheless. I deserved it. I knew better than to touch someone's private property without asking. This was precisely why he should've had his catalog behind bullet-proof glass.

Mr. Lear smiled.

"Oh, hi," I said, relaxed like he was my Uncle Norman. "How's it going?"

"Good," he answered, matching my relaxed tone. Did *he* think he was my uncle?

"Would you like to see the rest of the house?"

"Sure, if you're not too busy."

The couple in the corner stopped arguing long enough to hear Mr. Lear's offer and cozied up to us. *Sure, now that I laid the groundwork, hop on my coattails, why don't you.* Maybe Mr. Lear's offer was meant for anyone in earshot, but I like to think he singled me out.

We followed Mr. Lear up the main staircase with a white metal railing wound around the Rodin tower. I stuck close to him, like a duckling imprinting onto its mother. I was transfixed by his unruffled demeanor. When the time was right, I wanted to ask him whose idea it was for Sammy Davis Jr. to kiss Archie Bunker in the smooch seen around the world in 1972.

We reached the second-floor balcony. It offered the most spectacular views of the ocean and the city. The three of us oohed and aahed. Mr. Lear told us he was rebuilding parts of his house that had sustained damage from the 1994 Northridge earthquake. Oh, I could relate to that. It was four in the morning when the earthquake hit. In our apartment in West Los Angeles, my husband and I had huddled naked in a fetal position in an arched doorway for safety. I have no idea where that advice came from. Squinting, I'd looked over my knees into our dining room. The large pie cabinet was on its side, and VHS tapes and dominos were scattered everywhere. I wondered if the Lears had huddled naked in one of their doorways.

Mr. Lear said he was extending the driveway during the rebuild.

"Extend?" I asked. "But it's already so long. Do you have to take a shuttle to the mailbox?"

Mr. Lear narrowed his eyes but didn't say anything. My pulse quickened, and I tasted bile in the back of my throat. The couple turned and scowled at me.

I wasn't trying to be funny. I was trying to neutralize my excitement. I couldn't express the true extent of my child-like glee. I didn't want him to think I was a star-fucker. But the more I tried to act calm, the more desperate for attention I looked. In that moment, there wasn't any difference between me and Norman Lear. We were both admiring the vistas and the Pacific Ocean. But really, I thought I'd shit my pants.

We walked through a windowed breezeway. Directly below was a swimming pool with a blue plastic slide. Mr. Lear led us into the connecting room, which was his office. Shiny Peabody awards, Golden Globes, and Emmys surrounded me. Covering a large ebony desk were framed photos of family and friends—friends like Milton Berle and Gandhi.

I wasn't paying attention to where I was standing, and when I moved slightly to my right, I nearly knocked over a table littered with stacks of books—so many titles containing the word "death"—*and* another hat. I had a strong impulse to try it on. It wasn't such a far-fetched idea, him being my uncle and all. But then I thought better of it. Instead, I folded my arms across my chest and pinned them to my ribs in case one of my hands went rogue.

My mouth was about to betray me—I could feel it. Thoughts started revving. Words were falling over themselves, pushing past good sense and self-control, picking up speed, and racing toward my lips. I motioned toward his desk. "So this is where the magic happens, huh." I realize (now) how unoriginal this statement is. But at the time, I thought I was friggin' Mark Twain.

A hush fell over the room; anticipation hung in the air. I begged for the antler chandelier to fall on my head. My heart thumped in my ears. I looked over at Mr. Lear, who pierced me with his blue eyes. The moment felt thrillingly dangerous, and I wished for a trap door beneath my feet.

"Funny, kid. That was funny." I was definitely going to shit my pants.

It was a seminal exchange for me. I don't presume to know what it meant to Norman Lear. I'd experienced nothing but rejection for the past seven years in Los Angeles. His compliment was the most significant I'd received to date. Praise from my gynecologist, who I make laugh every time her face is in my crotch, didn't count.

With those five words, I felt acknowledged and validated. "Comedy is your destiny," he was saying. "It hasn't been a waste of time. Sure, the odds are against you, but never give up. You got it, kid."

I'd made Norman Lear laugh, and I rode the victory for a long time. It was a win in an often callous industry. It might've been the last victory for a while, so I bragged to anyone and everyone who let me. Unfortunately, my husband got the bulk of it.

A few days later, Lori called and thanked me for coming to her party.

"Hey, Norman wants to know if you've written for television."

After I came to, I lied. "Yes." At that time, the only television experience I had was watching it. And the only writing I was doing was for my fledgling stand-up act—my latest endeavor. Apparently, misery and long shots are a turn-on.

"He wants to bring you in to discuss a project. Call his office." I copied the number on another blue Post-it note with the precision of a plastic surgeon.

The Aristophanes of sitcoms had asked for me! What was I supposed to do? Tell the truth? Politely pass on the invitation?! I couldn't let pesky facts like inexperience or unpreparedness stop me. It was an offer I couldn't refuse. Sure, I was shocked, nervous, and scared, but none of it mattered. This was "it."

Details aside, I was now a TV comedy writer.

One week later, I was in Mr. Lear's office in a nondescript building in Culver City. A woman, whose hair bun was the tightest I'd ever seen, holding several files against her chest, greeted me at the elevator. She introduced herself as a production assistant and offered me a bottle of Evian water. *Sweet.*

Hair Bun escorted me into a conference room, where Mr. Lear and his partner, whose name escapes me, were seated around a large table. We shook hands, and again, I had to suppress my giggles when I saw Mr. Lear in his hat.

"So, tell us about yourself," the partner said, "and your writing experience."

Writing experience? He caught me off-guard, which was friggin' idiotic. His question was the most obvious and logical he could ask. My whole body felt like it was on fire. I flipped through my resume in my head. Um, gofer on the movie *Can You Feel Me Dancing* ten years prior? Stage managing the play *A Shayna Maidel* at the Jewish Community Center in Seattle? I threw out a few stale tidbits that seemed to keep them interested.

"I've always wanted to write." (Lie.) "Actually, I worked for a writing team last year. It was a great learning experience." No, it wasn't—unless you consider learning how to print double-sided scripts experience.

I didn't directly answer the producer's question. Instead, the question became an ominous hum that droned in my ears the entire time I was in the office.

Mr. Lear slid a television script across the table. "We want to get ideas on improving the story. How we can punch it up and make it funnier."

I picked up the script and read the title: *Lady Peggy*.

"Are you interested in reading it and giving us your take?" Mr. Lear asked. He said it with deference that should have been reserved for someone with a mountain of notable credits—or any credits.

"Sure. I'd love to." My only option was to say yes. It didn't matter that a rash spread across my chest and I developed a sudden lisp. I couldn't come clean without admitting that I'd tried to trick everyone. The thought of Mr. Lear feeling like he'd made a mistake was inconceivable.

I'll take "fake it till I make it" for two hundred, Alex.

"We're talking to Blaine Walker to direct the pilot," Mr. Lear offered. "He's a pain in the ass, but his work on *Crazy 'bout the Barber* was glorious."

"I loved that show," I chimed. "I'm not usually a fan of multi-camera sitcoms. They always look artificial." And then it occurred to me that most of Norman's shows were multicamera sitcoms.

Mr. Lear and his partner nodded to each other. "We'll be using a multicamera setup for this show if it gets picked up."

"Right, obviously. It's worked out for you." Quitting while ahead isn't a concept I'm well-versed in. "I don't have to tell you," I continued, "filming in front of a studio audience is like doing a play. The immediate reaction from an audience that actors love. Yup, that would be my preference too." My head was so far up my ass that my only hope was to suffocate.

The men continued telling me about their vision for the project. But it was amateur hour, evidenced by my blank and lifeless stare. I waited for them to take-backsies on the script. But they didn't. I mustered what confidence I could and swallowed my self-doubt. I was sipping Evian water with Mr. Lear because of my two (seemingly) witty quips. He hadn't asked to see a writing sample, so I must've dazzled him with my winning personality. I had nothing to worry about.

Twenty minutes later, we stood, and I agreed to return in a week.

It was happening so fast. A chance encounter at a party— and bam! I'm creating a show with Norman Lear. It was all I'd ever wanted—a seat at the table. My dreams were coming true.

My corner office was within reach, my name on the door and an espresso machine in a hidden cabinet. I began to fantasize. I'll tell Norman about my performing aspirations. To which he'll respond, "No surprise after seeing your performance at my house." I'll costar in *Lady Peggy*. I'm sure she has a best friend. Then again, I'm also fond of bossing people around—maybe I'll direct season two.

The more possibilities I imagined, the more anxious I became. I cranked up the air-conditioning in my car to cool down the heat rash that was spreading along my arms. A high-profile collaboration with Mr. Lear would be time-consuming. I'd have to get used to a new work schedule—no more sleeping until eleven. My husband would have to take over dog-walking duties. How was I supposed to juggle running errands and notoriety? Photo shoots for billboard promos? Say goodbye to anonymity. Bye-bye in-person appearances at the post office and Trader Joe's. My marriage will likely suffer. I could get a divorce. Push comes to shove, I wasn't about to let something like marriage get in my way.

I also had to protect myself legally. When I shared my thoughts with Mr. Lear the following week, what would stop him from deciding not to hire me and stealing my ideas? I wouldn't be taken advantage of—not even by Mr. Norman Lear.

I pulled over and parked on a random side street in West Hollywood. I opened my Filofax (it was 1997) and called an entertainment lawyer friend of my family. "You're putting the cart before the horse," Martin said. I thought I heard him laugh. "Why don't you wait and see how it turns out? You know, we also represent Norman." I hoped that there wouldn't be a conflict of interest when Martin made our deals.

Either I presented with low self-esteem or I believed that I was this close to running Hollywood. There's no middle ground. No matter how delusional I might've been, I genuinely believed my crap. I wouldn't have gotten out of bed in the morning if I didn't. To a lesser extent, I still feel this way.

I spent the following week in a movie montage, which is how I understand my life, working on the script.

There I am, going in and out of coffee shops and libraries around Los Angeles. In one café, I hold a large coffee in one hand and a pen in the other, frozen, unable to write. And I'm crying. In another shot, I hike up a dirt trail in Runyon Canyon with Little Ricky. I shake my head, frustrated, and pull at my eyelashes. The creative juices just won't flow. Suddenly, bees start swarming around my head. I start running down the hill, dog in tow, swatting as I go. It only aggravates the bees, and they give chase. The final shot is at Silver Lake, where I wander around looking for inspiration in the faces of elderly speed walkers. I look creepy, staring at them through the mesh insect shield draped over my baseball cap—you don't have to tell me twice. The elderly walkers pick up their pace. I sit on a bench, dejected. "How can you be this empty and unimaginative?" I scream, scaring away a little kid on a skateboard. "Your lack of fresh ideas is stunning."

End of montage.

I returned to Norman Lear's office at our scheduled time. He and his partner sat in the same spot as in our first meeting. We exchanged a few pleasantries, and then it was showtime! A lot was riding on my feedback. And I really wanted to deliver the laughs—again. This break had to change my life. I wasn't sure how much more stamina and delusion I had left.

"The part where Peggy discovers she's not Frank's mother doesn't really work," I began. "It feels forced. Suppose she does bring the inflatable nativity scene when she visits her father on Christmas Eve. Wouldn't prison security check it first?" I thought I was being clever. Look at me. *I* know what's wrong with the story.

But that wasn't the assignment. I was only parroting what Mr. Lear and his partner had already established the week before. My job was to show them how to *fix* the problems. Unfortunately, I didn't realize any of this until it was too late. I'd already jumped off the cliff, so my humiliation continued.

"The dialogue can be funnier," I said with a straight face to the trailblazing creator of *All in the Family*. And instead of offering actual examples, I dribbled a buffet of half-baked suggestions. I grasped at anything I could to prove that I deserved to be there. And that I had something to offer. I wanted Norman Lear to take a chance on me.

I wiped beads of sweat from my upper lip with the back of my hand. *Where's Hair Bun with some goddamn Evian?*

To their credit, Mr. Lear and his partner listened without interrupting—or asking me to leave. Fifteen endless minutes later, it was over. The men smiled politely, but they didn't fool me. There was disappointment behind those smiles. They uttered a collective, "Okay, great." My performance was anything but. Not only was I a terrible actress and unable to fake it, but my winning personality couldn't save me either.

Norman Lear was all class. He was generous and stately and didn't make me feel like a moron. I'd taken care of that all by myself. I'd hoped to make the dreams of my younger (and current) self come true, but instead, I'd let Norman Lear down.

As crushed and embarrassed as I was, I wasn't ready for Norman Lear in 1997. But my belief then, as it is today, is to embrace every opportunity, even the outlandish ones, whether you're prepared or not, because you never know. Had I not accepted Mr. Lear's offer, I wouldn't have received a note from him later that week that did indeed change my career trajectory.

"This is going to take someone with a little more experience than just us three in the room—and if you have an idea, think of this as an open door—you are a delight."

His glowing endorsement and heartfelt appeal gave me the push I needed to pursue writing comedy. However, before I could even think about returning to the crime scene, I had to get experience. I wasn't about to let Mr. Lear down a second time.

But years later, even when I had a few professional credits and a filing cabinet full of show ideas, I still didn't reach out to Mr. Lear. Forcing him to put his money where his mouth was and collect on his "open door" offer was too big of an ask—and too scary. What if my writing still wasn't good enough? What if he'd never really meant the offer and was just trying to be polite? So much time had passed. Would he even remember me? I'd probably have to make a copy of his note and send it along as evidence. That would've been so lame and way beyond the humiliation I'd already endured.

Wow, I remember thinking then, *what happened to your chutzpah and your balls?* Maybe someone with a bigger set and greater confidence in their talents could've collected on Mr. Lear's offer. But unfortunately, that person wasn't me. As sorry as I am that I didn't grow a pair (I just want to see how many references to testes I can make in one paragraph), I'm thankful for my time with Norman. And I'd like to think that now, with my lived experience and maturity, if someone made me an offer as Mr. Lear did, I'd grab my now heavier filing cabinet and knock on their door without a moment's hesitation. Maybe.

seven

I Came Out of an Orthodox Jewish California Closet

WHEN I WAS STILL a nascent Pilates instructor, I was in my early forties, living with Julian in New Jersey. I worked in three studios, trying to cobble together a clientele and a steady paycheck. I did anything and everything I could to get experience. I cycled through a lot of different jobs in Los Angeles, and with each one, I started at the bottom. Paying dues was a part of the process, and Pilates wasn't any different. However, there was one incident in the early days that was a bridge too far.

On a hot and muggy morning, I walked into one of the studios where I worked, Pilates Mind and Movement. Ellen Wilson, the studio owner, was jumping on a mini trampoline. I looked away. She was going to fling herself headfirst into the rack of dumbbells—I just knew it. She wasn't wearing a supportive sports bra, and when you're that top-heavy and refuse to harness that kind of weight, accidents can happen.

"Hey, can you cover a session for me on Thursday? Somehow, I double-booked," Ellen asked mid-jump. "It's with Aaron, one of my regulars."

"Sure," I said. It was nice to have her approval.

Come Thursday, Aaron Meyers entered the studio wearing a long black coat over a black suit and a tall fur hat. And when he removed his hat, there was a yarmulke bobby pinned to the crown of his head. Knotted fringes from a tallit, or prayer shawl, hung down under his shirt. Ellen hadn't mentioned that Aaron was an Orthodox Jew. Not that it would've mattered, but it caught me off guard. I hoped my bug-eyed expression wouldn't betray my surprise or be perceived as discriminatory. You can't be too careful these days.

Obviously, fitness and working out don't discriminate. But there weren't many (or any) Orthodox Jews jogging on the boardwalk in my neighborhood or doing tricep dips on the bike racks in the park. Nor had I ever seen Orthodox Jews exercising in movies, in TV shows, or on Broadway.

Everything I know about Judaism, Orthodox or otherwise, can fit in a toy dreidel. And that information came from the musicals *Jesus Christ Superstar* and *Yentl*. My dad tried to educate my brother and me about our history and culture when we were young, seeing as knowledge and history were like my dad's party drugs. We celebrated traditional Jewish holidays and were dragged to temple every year for the high holidays, Rosh Hashanah and Yom Kippur. As teenagers, my brother and I begged our parents to leave us at home. We were uninterested in anything that took us away from our tragically important lives, which consisted of sitting around with friends, playing video games, or, in my case, convincingly acting the part of a partially blind scientist.

My dad would yell, beads of sweat clinging to his mustache, "I ask one thing from you two, and this is what I get?" As our punishment, we'd be forced to sit in the first row, where Rabbi Stern and God could keep an eye on us.

"Hi, Aaron," I said. "It's nice to meet you."

"Hello." He breezed past me, avoiding eye contact, and disappeared into the bathroom.

When he reemerged, he was wearing what I believed he believed were workout clothes: a white sleeveless undershirt, black suit pants, and black knee socks. He made a beeline for the reformer machine and lay down without my prompting. I stood behind the foot bar at the end of the machine, hovering over Aaron's raggedy black socks. I tried not to, but I couldn't help staring at him. This uber-religious man looking up at me was intimidating. Suddenly, he was radioactive. I moved back an inch, unsure what to do. Then, I remembered my training and asked him a few diagnostic questions. "Do you have any injuries or limitations I should know about?"

"My lower back is tight, but no injuries," Aaron answered. He didn't seem rattled by my presence in the slightest. And why would he? He'd been training with Ellen for years. The weirdness was coming from me.

"Is it okay if I touch you?" I asked. "To adjust for alignment." My question sounded pervy.

"Sure, you can touch me," Aaron answered. And then he sounded pervy.

After that exchange, I couldn't stop thinking about accidentally touching Aaron in his neyn-neyn place, his customs, my lack of customs, Jewish people in general, and Jewish sex in particular. Ah!

Not long after I became an instructor, my first male client was an English professor in his fifties. I was still getting used to touching a man in a nonsexual and professional way. He came to his session wearing loose-fitting sateen running shorts straight out of a 1982 high school gym class. He was lying on the reformer with his feet in the loops (which are attached to springs), making wide circles, when one of his balls slid out of his shorts. I didn't know whether to laugh or cry. I pretended someone was calling my name from across the room and looked away. My only hope was that he'd quickly corral the boys back in the barn. Which he thankfully did. The second time one of his nads went astray, he was lying on the mat with both of his legs spread over his head. I wished he wasn't so proud of his flexibility. I waited. And when I couldn't take it any longer, I motioned toward his deserter. *Do you need a hand?*

Aaron pushed the reformer's carriage up and back with his legs while I counted his reps out loud. I couldn't quite put my finger on it, but teaching Aaron didn't feel right. Kind of like how I felt about living in New Jersey.

Why shouldn't, or wouldn't, Orthodox Jews care about their health? Was I judging? Did I have dopey preconceptions? I knew nothing about this community. Happy, Dad?

There was little conversation during the session, which was a blessing. I put Aaron on different pieces of equipment, where he proceeded to pull, push, bend, and extend. Fifty-five minutes later, it was over.

Aaron walked back into the bathroom. And I wiped down the equipment to prepare for my next client. Minutes later, he reappeared wearing his long black coat over his black suit and fur hat.

Just looking at him made me sweat—it was the middle of July. He stopped and turned to me on his way out.

"Can you come to my house and give my wife, Rachael, and me private lessons?"

"Sure." I didn't even hesitate. It was my first such request, and it felt swanky.

After eight months of teaching, I was ready to level up. First, suburban New Jersey, then private jets to private islands with my Pilates magic circle and expertise on board.

When I got home that night, I called my dad and told him about Aaron. For reasons that now escape me, I thought he'd be interested.

"Are you sure he's Orthodox?" my dad asked.

"What do you mean?" His question irritated me. Why was he quizzing me as if he didn't trust that I knew what a yarmulke and a fur hat represented? Although I couldn't really blame him, based on my history. Still.

"I'm asking," my dad explained, "because the Orthodox forbid unrelated men and women to touch unless it's with a spouse or a close family member."

"I knew something wasn't kosher!" We laughed.

"So it's odd he's exercising with you," my dad continued. "Women are considered temptations and distractions."

"Okay, Dad." I thought I heard him removing the Talmud from the shelf in his library. I'd get an earful of quotes and commandments if I didn't hang up. "I have to go. Bye."

Great, Aaron didn't consider me a temptation or a distraction. That was depressing. Sinful or not. First, the boys in high school, and now Aaron.

A week later, I drove to Aaron and Rachael's house in Lakewood in the early morning. The town has a large Orthodox Jewish community. I squeezed my MINI Cooper into the only available space, between a fleet of Dodge Caravans and vintage Buick station wagons. Red and yellow plastic cars and bicycles littered the neighborhood yards and driveways, including the Meyers'.

I stepped out of my car, clutching various props under my arms. Just then, a school bus arrived and double-parked in front of me, blocking my path. I waited while adorable boys with side curls and backpacks ran out of the houses and climbed aboard. When the bus drove off, I continued walking, balancing, and trying not to faceplant as I hopscotched around a scooter to the Meyers' front door.

Aaron greeted me wearing black drawstring sweatpants and a white sleeveless undershirt like the one he'd worn in the Pilates studio, only this one had bits of his breakfast on it. He had one arm propped up on the doorframe and the other on the doorknob. He reminded me of Stanley Kowalski from *A Streetcar Named Desire*—if Stanley had a long, full beard and a skullcap.

"Come in," Aaron said, turning away, avoiding eye contact again.

"Good morning," I answered, probably too perky for the early hour.

Aaron immediately started up the front staircase. "Follow me."

There was an air of familiarity that I wasn't altogether comfortable with. I followed Aaron with a mix of curiosity and vigilance.

Hanging on the wall along the staircase were billboard-size photos of six Meyers children—all under the age of seven, I'm guessing. I have no idea what kids are supposed to look like at what ages. I am, however, reasonably confident that my parents love my brother and me, and when we were kids, wallet-size photos of us were big enough. One stairway billboard was of a doe-eyed boy with long, wavy, dirty blond hair wearing a tie-dye yarmulke. I stifled a laugh. I expected to see school pictures of the kids (the boys anyway) at their desks at the Yeshiva, not looking like someone shrunk Matthew McConaughey.

To the right of the landing was a long hallway with several doors on either side. Undoubtedly, one of them was the tricked-out home gym. Aaron approached the door nearest us and banged on it. "Hannah," he yelled. "Breakfast is ready. Go downstairs and join your mother." There was no response.

Aaron turned back toward me. "This way," he said and then continued in the opposite direction of Hannah's room. *Where are we going?* I was already self-conscious about fraternizing with a half-naked Orthodox Jewish man. And now I felt like I was on *Let's Make a Deal.* Do I want to know what's behind door number two?

We stopped in front of some double doors at the end of the hallway—a dead end. Aaron turned the doorknob and pushed. *Why in the name of Abraham is he showing me his bedroom?* Grisly imaginings tumbled over themselves in my head. *Maybe this in-home Pilates session is a ruse. Maybe it's actually an abduction. What if Aaron is a member of some freaky Orthodox sex ring and he's going to have his way with me?* And then I thought about Rachael. She wouldn't let anything happen to me—certainly not in her bedroom. *But what if he got rid of Rachael because he thought I was a temptress and a distraction after all? What if I was the other woman? And now his children were motherless, and he needed me to fill Rachael's wig.*

My cheeks flushed. Aaron and I stood in his bedroom doorway, staring at his boxer shorts on the handlebars of an exercise bike from the 1970s. The Meyers were my first in-home private clients. How could I ask any questions and demand answers? I didn't want to be rude. I was probably overreacting. But then I reasoned that overreacting was better than dying. I was confident I could strangle him using the fringes on his prayer shawl, if needed.

Two twin beds lined the far wall, with a nightstand separating them. The sheets were untucked and tangled inside the blankets. A Star of David clock and a framed ketubah (a marriage contract) hung on the walls. The whole thing was bizarre and incredibly awkward.

Aaron pointed to an open door opposite the twin beds. "In there."

Huh?!

He made his way to the door, and I slowly made my way to Aaron—like a lamb to the slaughter.

We walked into a thoughtfully appointed California Closet. I couldn't stop staring at the precision organization. The closet gave new meaning to the phrase "a place for everything and everything in its place." White cotton robes (or kittels) hung on multiple metal rungs below rows of neatly arranged flat-topped fur hats. A selection of women's wigs mounted on Styrofoam heads sat on an enormous center island. It looked like the costume department for the Netflix show *Shtisel*. It made me lightheaded to be within spitting distance of the Meyers' religious clothing.

"Will this work?" Aaron asked, standing under a tiny window.

For what? I thought. And then it hit me.

Aaron wanted to do Pilates in the closet for reasons unknown to me then—and now. His tone and unkempt eyebrows were pretty persuasive. It didn't sound like his question was up for discussion.

As far as I'm concerned, the only reason to work in a closet is if you're constructing it. As shocked and tongue-tied as I was, I wanted the private jet and private island clientele. If this was what it took, then so be it. I was paying my dues.

I turned away from Aaron to gather myself. And there was Rachael, in the corner of the closet, lying on a tattered loveseat, breastfeeding a baby. I'd been so flustered by Aaron's request that I'd overlooked the mother and child.

Rachael and I locked eyes. If she was surprised to see me, she didn't show it. What was so crazy about the three of us—excuse me, the four of us—tucked snuggly in their closet was that neither of them acknowledged we were even in a closet! They'd clearly discussed the arrangement before I arrived because no one ever said "closet."

"Hi," I said, smiling, trying to avoid looking at Rachael's exposed nipple.

"Hi. Nice to meet you," Rachael said. "This is Levi."

Aaron had told me that Rachael recently gave birth, but he hadn't said just how recently.

"Maybe I should come back when you finish with the, um . . ." I nodded toward Rachael's breast. How could she not want privacy? I wanted privacy.

"That's okay," Aaron interjected. "I'll go first."

I asked him if he had a yoga mat.

"I don't think so," he mumbled. "You didn't bring one?"

I'd brought foam rollers, squishy balls, and elastic bands, but no mat. I'd assumed that he'd have one in his tricked-out home gym. I would've gladly brought one had he asked me to.

Rachael stood and handed Levi to Aaron. "I may have one," she said, exiting the closet.

She returned with a yoga mat. "It's from that one class I took two years ago." Rachael took Levi from Aaron and lay back on the loveseat, picking up where they'd left off.

Aaron crouched down on the floor and lay his six-foot frame onto the mat, his feet hanging off the end. I watched him shift and adjust, trying to find a comfortable configuration. But it was pointless—the mat wouldn't suddenly grow five inches.

"Are you married?" Aaron asked, rolling up from the floor and touching his toes.

Why was he talking? We didn't chitchat in the studio.

"I live with my boyfriend," I said. "He's Catholic." I hoped it would end the conversation right there.

"Oh," Aaron said. "Have you ever been married?"

"Actually, I'm divorced." I instructed Aaron to start his single-leg circles. "He was Jewish."

"Did you get a Get?" he asked.

"Did I get a what?" I repeated.

"A Get."

"Did I get a Get?"

"Yes, did your husband give you a Get?"

It went on like this for a few rounds, like the Abbott and Costello skit "Who's on First?"

When I got home later that day, I googled "Get." According to Jewish law, a Get ends a marriage—it's a divorce document. For those of you wondering, I did not get a Get. What I got was a hundred-dollar divorce courtesy of the folks at We the People in Riverside, California.

Rachael watched Aaron and me while Levi drank his breakfast. My voice slightly shook while I put Aaron through his paces. I wasn't used to teaching in front of an audience and I was nervous. And I was laying my hands on Aaron in front of his wife and baby in their closet. I felt like a Jezebel. I was definitely breaking centuries-old laws. If word ever got out, I'd be stoned at the hands of their congregation for sure. But when I looked over at Rachael and then at Aaron, they didn't seem bothered by any of it.

Maybe Aaron and Rachael had a good reason for closet Pilates. I just couldn't imagine what it was. Maybe I was being too rigid. Maybe working out in unconventional spaces was common in Pilates. Who was I to say where people should and should not work out? I was a beginner, after all. I just wasn't sure that I'd be able to do my job to the best of my ability in a closet. I also didn't want to make a fuss or embarrass anyone. So I sat in humiliating silence, teaching Pilates to an Orthodox Jewish couple inside their California Closet.

When my time with Aaron ended, I asked to use the bathroom. He walked me to the back of the closet and into a connected bathroom. The door was missing, and the toilet was hidden behind a half wall. *What?! Did Julian and Aaron compare bathroom/bedroom floor plans?*

"I had it remodeled as a gift for Rachael," Aaron boasted. "It's not finished; you can use the bathroom in the hall."

I was still recovering from the Pilates-lactation lounge and was too distracted to hear what Aaron said. And when he didn't leave the bathroom, I thought he planned to stay while I peed. If hanging out in the closet was acceptable to him, it wasn't a giant leap to hanging out in the bathroom with your Pilates instructor. For a second there, I thought I'd allow it—I didn't want to be disrespectful.

"I'll be out in a minute," I squeaked. Aaron turned and left.

Only after I sat down did what Aaron said about using another bathroom register. He'd hesitated to leave because he didn't think I'd stay. He was waiting for *me* to walk out.

Back in the closet, I prayed I wouldn't have to teach Rachael with Levi latched on to her nipple. Fortunately, she was alone.

"Ready?" I asked, forcing a smile.

"I don't really want to do this; it's my husband's idea."

It was so honest. And it made me wonder if Aaron was body-shaming Rachael into getting her pre-pregnancy body back.

"Let's go slow and see how you feel." It would've been easy to let Rachael off the hook. But I wouldn't abandon ship. I was a profes-sional. A professional teaching in a closet. Never mind.

"I hardly ever work out," Rachael moaned, lifting her hips into a bridge.

"Really?" I said.

"Do you have any children?" Rachael asked.

"Not that I'm aware of," I answered, joking. "I don't believe in them." And then I remembered the wall of photos. "Not that there's anything wrong with kids."

I pivoted. "How's your general health?"

"Fine, I guess." Her energy was making me drowsy.

"How old is Levi?"

"Three weeks."

My face dropped. "Should you be working out?"

"I don't know."

"Did your doctor tell you it was okay?" I asked.

"I don't know. I never asked her."

I panicked. I wouldn't have had Rachael do any abdominal

exercises had I known it'd only been three weeks. What if I damaged her? That wouldn't be a good look for me or my fledgling business.

When I looked up the information later that day, I learned that six weeks is the suggested time women should wait before resuming physical activity after giving birth. It could be much longer after a C-section. I wasn't about to ask Rachael how Levi came out of her. Instead, I told her I'd wait for her doctor to clear her before we continued.

We exited the closet and tiptoed through the bedroom, passing Levi's crib. Rachael walked me to the door and stopped at the threshold, as if the hallway contained hidden land mines.

"Aaron will be downstairs shortly, and he'll pay you," she whispered and then turned her back and shut the door. It was so matter of fact. After all we'd been through, she could have told me to have a nice day. And to trust me to wait downstairs unsupervised was odd. I thought about swiping some of her silver teacups from the hutch to teach her a lesson. Instead, I waited in their front hallway under the watchful gaze of all her children's billboards.

At last, Aaron appeared and handed me a check. "How did it go?"

"Well, Rachael told me that she doesn't have permission from her doctor to exercise."

"Don't worry, she'll have it by next week when you come back."

Aaron slammed the front door behind me, nearly clipping the end of my foam roller.

A couple of days later, I was teaching in one of my other studios, and I bumped into Beth, a fellow instructor. I thought about asking her if she'd ever encountered a situation like the one I had with Aaron and Rachael. And then I thought, which situation specifically? Teaching in a California Closet? Stretching a new mother's abdominals like a rubber band? And then I remembered what happened the last time I engaged Beth in a professional conversation. It was my first week of teaching, and I wanted to know how she dealt with female clients who came to the studio with unshaven legs, calluses, and corns. I argued that they created hazardous work conditions, and it was gross. "You wouldn't go to your gynecologist without grooming, would you?" I'd asked her. "It's just common courtesy. My clients should think of me as their pilatescologist." She'd called me intolerant and stomped off. The next time my client put her feet up on the reformer and flecks of skin fell to the floor like she was molting, I sucked it up—my disgust, not the skin.

In the end, I decided it was probably best for everyone if I didn't share my closet escapades with Beth.

Rachael's doctor cleared her for Pilates, but my relationship with the Meyers deteriorated. They repeatedly canceled without the mandated twenty-four-hour notice and were late with payments. I thought I had to be grateful for the work—no matter what or where it took place. But it'd gotten ridiculous, and three months later, I decided to quit.

Just before noon on a Tuesday, I rang the Meyers' doorbell one last time, feeling good, feeling strong. I'd psyched myself up. *They don't deserve my hard work and commitment. And I'm not going back in the closet.*

"Hello? Hello?" Rachael's raspy voice blared through a tiny speaker on the wall next to the doorbell.

I pushed the intercom button. "It's me."

"I just woke up. Please wait. Or let yourself in."

"Okay, I'll wait here." I didn't want to let myself in.

Ten minutes passed before Rachael appeared at the door. She was wearing a loosely tied robe, and I could see the top of a pale green nightgown underneath. Her long, natural chestnut hair was matted against her face like a used dryer sheet stuck on a towel.

"Sorry, I didn't hear my alarm go off. I have to get dressed. Come in."

I wondered what she'd been doing while I was outside. And then I thought about Levi. I was thankful I didn't have to dine with the two of them again.

When Rachael was dressed, I followed her into her bedroom, stopping short of the closet. "Why don't we work out here?" I suggested, knowing this was my last day. "You'll have more room."

"Okay." Rachael lowered herself gingerly onto the mat. Was it this easy? Why didn't I speak up sooner?

"I'm just so exhausted all the time," Rachael sighed.

I was genuinely sorry if Aaron was forcing her to work with me. But her indifference didn't do anything for my self-esteem. Teaching her wasn't fun—it felt like I was doing math. And it wasn't benefiting her either. I was supposed to be a good thing in her life, but I felt more like a bother and an inconvenience.

Per my instructions, she attempted to lift her head and shoulders off the mat.

"How's Levi?" I asked, trying to distract her. "I can't imagine the challenges with a newborn in addition to your other kids." And then it dawned on me. I'd never seen the other kids.

Levi started wailing from the crib.

"I'm done," Rachael announced resignedly.

It'd been less than twenty-five minutes. And even though I'd decided only to give the bare minimum, I felt deflated. I excused myself and went to the bathroom—the one with a proper door and a lock.

When I returned to the bedroom, Rachael was in bed snoring.

"In here," a voice bellowed from the closet. I knew that voice. It was Aaron. And I went to him, convinced I was suffering from Stockholm syndrome.

"We were out late last night," Aaron crowed, nodding in Rachael's direction. "At a party until three in the morning."

"Wow."

He may have still been drunk because he was unusually friendly. He set his yoga mat down under the tiny window like always, and I didn't stop him.

I loved my work, and I wanted others to love it, but Aaron and Rachael sucked the joy right out.

"My fifty-year-old sister-in-law got engaged," Aaron continued, holding a plank. "You see, it's not too late." I made him hold a plank for five minutes until his body shook and he couldn't keep his head up and sweat rained down on the mat. What?

When we finished, we stood in the bedroom side by side, staring at the blankets moving on Rachael's bed. Her head was buried under a pillow, but her bottom was lifted toward the sky.

I cleared my throat and turned to Aaron. "This is our last session. I won't be coming back."

Aaron shrugged his shoulders. "Okay."

He clearly wasn't broken up about my departure, and his apathy felt like a slap in the face. First, Aaron didn't consider me a turn-on or a diversion, and now he didn't care that I wouldn't be returning. *Do I mean nothing to you?!*

I left the bedroom, hurried downstairs, threw the last of the silver teacups into my bag, and showed myself out.

You might think that would've been the end of it. You know, lessons learned and all. But several days later, I received a phone call from Rachael's friend, Naomi, asking me for an in-home private lesson. I thought the community deserved a second chance. Why should one effed-up encounter spoil it for everyone? I was optimistic that this time would be different.

My sessions with Naomi took place in her basement. We set up a mat in the middle of a jungle gym surrounded by toy building blocks. Her three-legged dachshund, Mike, watched over us. And like clockwork, midway through each session, her feral toddler twin boys would barge in, interrupt my brilliant and inspired teaching, cutting the session short. After the fourth time, I quit. It was *farkakteh*!

It hadn't been my life that was in jeopardy back in Aaron's closet; it was my self-respect. Clearly, I wasn't destined to be the Orthodox Jewish community's go-to Pilates instructor. I'm not going to lie; it hurt. And I was disappointed. I had such high hopes. But any thoughts I had of flying to private islands in private jets to teach private Pilates sessions vanished—at least in this community.

However, there was some good that came out of the experiences. Aaron, Rachael, and Naomi showed me that I (still) had some work to do on speaking up for myself. Forget about nobody putting Dani in a corner. *Nobody* puts Dani in a closet.

eight

Revenge Travel

IF YOU ASK MY FRIENDS or family if they think I'm a vengeful person, I'm almost certain they'd say no. Whenever I feel slighted or treated unfairly, revenge isn't my first stop. Nope, that honor goes to acting like a petty cunt. This isn't to say I'm incapable of retaliating, because I am. But, generally speaking, my vengeance is bubble-wrapped and tucked under my bed. I keep it sandwiched between the chips from my shoulder that I was able to knock off and an assortment of grudges and resentments. But when Julian broke up with me after seven years together, I was provoked, and pettiness just wasn't enough.

Shortly after the breakup, I was on the phone with Julian's daughter, Nicole, now nineteen years old—she, Tyler, and I stayed in touch because we didn't break up with each other, and I loved them—when she mentioned in passing that her father was in Barcelona with his new girlfriend. The girlfriend that he'd cheated on me with. It'd only been three months since we split up. I remember

when I found out about the infidelity. One shouldn't leave birthday cards from secret lovers lying around like dirty underwear.
The shock and fury were like none I'd ever experienced—or care
to experience ever again. Julian was an exceptional liar. And a way
better actor than I ever was.

If you travel with your hussy as if traveling wasn't our thing,
do I not protest? If you insult me with a companion fare for your
harlot, am I not quick to anger? If you mock me with a TSA Pre-
Check, do I not gasp for air? And if you poison our past, shall I not
seek retribution? How could I let him get away with such a blatant
betrayal? Julian used to think it was adorable how animated I got
over fresh passport stamps. No doubt he now stood by this floozy's
side, watching her get stamped.

As if the lies weren't devastating enough, but then to take his
floozy to Spain, where we'd gone together the year before? Where I
gleefully watched him eat pulled pork while this vegetarian nibbled
on seasonal roots and nuts? It was a twist of the knife that was still
lodged in my heart. Traveling was one of the few passions he and
I shared—the others being watching *The Voice* and having sex, not
necessarily in that order. In hindsight, I should've known that a
relationship can't survive on fornicating and singing alone.

There should've been a moratorium on suitcases and itineraries
for at least five years. I didn't think I had to spell it out for him. I
was picking shards of treason from my ass while he was strolling
carefree on Las Ramblas, stuffing his piehole with paella.

I tore into the bubble wrap under my bed, and revenge travel
was born.

I wouldn't stop moving until I collected so many stamps that
I'd need extra pages in my passport. I'd travel farther, faster, and first

class (if I could) to cities, countries, continents. I'd make revenge travel my job, which was convenient because I was between writing gigs. I'd cover the world map with colorful push pins. Now, all I had to do was turn off *Antiques Roadshow*, climb out from under the coffee table, and shower.

"It'll be a good distraction," my friend Melissa said on the phone one afternoon. She'd invited me to a yoga retreat she was leading in Sayulita, Mexico. As a Pilates instructor, I would've preferred a Pilates retreat, but I couldn't look a gift horse in the mouth. The itinerary was set, which meant little to no thinking or planning needed on my part. It was an opportunity to leave the house and start revenging. It would be my maiden voyage. I would show Julian that our breakup hadn't destroyed me or my lust for travel. I didn't ask her to, but I was confident that Nicole (who was now secretly my informant—unbeknownst to her) would leak information of my whereabouts to her dad. And when he heard, he'd feel the same razor-sharp cut of abandonment that I had.

Melissa continued. "All you have to do is send me the money and show up. You're going to love the food and the surfing. You surf, right?"

"Not after I nearly drowned in Puerto Rico with Julian," I hmphed. We had one lesson, which was briefer than a sneeze, before the instructor guided us out into the ocean. Within seconds, we were pulled under by violent waves and tossed around like rag dolls. When we finally came up for air, we had to paddle for half an hour before we could drag our limp bodies onto land.

"Okay," Melissa laughed. "No surfing. There are plenty of other things to do."

Melissa was laying it on thick, but my middle finger was pointed at Julian, so "Yes!" I shouted into the phone.

A month later, I was on a plane to Mexico for four days of retreating. A woman and her Chihuahua service dog sat beside me. I'm not a big fan of flying. There's usually a lot of deep breathing and fist-clenching. My seatmate didn't seem to be in any noticeable distress behind her copy of *Vanity Fair* despite the turbulence. I stared into the Chihuahua's round, milky eyes, hoping it would comfort me. It didn't.

When the local airport terminal came into focus, it looked like a bus stop—a short wooden bench with a corrugated metal sheet above it. The open-air ticket counter was a music stand. The Chihuahua and I trembled and whimpered as we touched down.

When I arrived at the resort, I was greeted by the owner, a man dressed in a white kaftan and wearing a White Sox baseball hat. Clearly, a tourist from Chicago had left it behind.

"The main building was constructed without machinery," he told me proudly. "Don't flush your used toilet paper," he added. "Throw it in the wastepaper basket." Who's going to know if I don't? Does an alarm go off? Will the resort police knock on my hand-built, sustainable cabana door and force me to fish out my used paper?

It'd been four years since I last saw Melissa. We met at a fitness studio in Dubai, where I taught Pilates and she taught yoga. She's one of the few people I know who give great hugs—no tentative side-ribcage bump, but a full-frontal, ten-second squeeze. I needed all the hugs I could get. We sat in the dining room and caught up while eating fruit I'd never heard of and couldn't pronounce. I updated her on all the unflattering details about my ex. She listened and offered compassion and assurance that the retreat was exactly what I needed. "It'll get your mind off him." I wanted to believe her. And for a while, I did.

After lunch, we walked down an unpaved trail to our shared cabana and dressed for our evening yoga class. The cabana wasn't equipped with electricity or internet. I was more than willing to unplug. It was a cozy room with oil lamps, candles, and mosquito netting draped over two twin beds. There were three solid walls and one open side, which faced the ocean. At night, we lowered gauzy curtains to cover the exposed side. I worried how flimsy fabric would keep out the shrieking wildlife in the trees and imagined a chachalaca snatching me from my bed in the middle of the night. Have you seen their talons? They're like Edward's scissorhands!

Midway through the evening yoga class, I wanted to hurl myself off the bamboo shala and into the hillside. How many downward dogs can there be in one class? If Melissa referred to my third eye one more time, I was going to tackle her on her sticky mat. I'll go out on a limb here and say I was downright belligerent. I'd tainted the whole session with breakup stink. But before I rushed the stage, Melissa bowed and whispered, "Namaste," signaling the end of class. I'd never been bored or anxious doing yoga. I'd certainly never wanted to hurt anyone while doing crow pose. It was a stinging reminder of just how badly broken my heart was.

I tried to tamp down my irritations in bed that night, but it was useless. They were suffocating me—just like the goddamn mosquito netting. The netting was doing its job of keeping out the mosquitos, but at the same time, it was also keeping out air. Barely twelve hours had passed since my arrival in Mexico, and I thought that maybe I was too hasty in agreeing to this trip. I wasn't ready to be in harmony with Mother Nature. If she were an actual person, I would've punched her in the face and kicked her in the shins.

I untied the mosquito netting, stumbled into the bathroom, and sat on the toilet. Warm liquid trickled down my legs. "Goddamn it!" I screamed.

"Are you okay?" Melissa yelled from her bed.

I was sitting on top of the seat cover. "I'm fine. I just peed myself."

In the morning, I skipped poolside yoga for obvious reasons. It was a new day and another chance to give my heartsick and grumpy demeanor some well-earned time off. I took a walk. I found a mountain of boulders that formed a sheltered cove along the coastline and started climbing. When I reached the top, I looked around for a place to sit. The only semi-flat surface was between two jagged rocks. I wobbled and shimmied until I felt balanced and centered. Clear blue skies above, a still ocean below, and a white sandy beach. By all accounts, this was postcard paradise. But I was too preoccupied wondering what Julian was doing to notice much of anything. Every time I'd shove him from my thoughts, it wasn't long before he slithered back in. I cursed him out from my perch, releasing a deluge of off-color insults and obscenities. I concluded by blaming myself for being so naïve.

When I got bored of feeling sorry for myself, I scanned the magnificent horizon. It would've been irresponsible not to take advantage of my surroundings. So I created a movie montage.

"Swing Low, Sweet Chariot" plays. My lover is dead. Family and friends arrive at my house for a memorial service. One by one, they surround me, enveloping me in their plump maternal arms, consoling, weeping. They offer support and fill my refrigerator with homemade dinners packed in Tupperware. Many tofu lasagnas and crudité are brought. I think, *Yay, I don't have to cook.* But after a while, I need some fresh air, and "I vant to be alone." So I stroll along the beach and find my way to this mound of jagged rocks. A breeze gently blows strands of hair across my face and some stick to my top lip. Tears slowly cascade down my cheeks like a gentle rain. The song crescendos. "Swing low, sweet chariot coming for to carry me home." I stare out at the white caps. A pod of dolphins jumps and flips in a game of one-upmanship.

Unfortunately, the movie was abruptly cut short when my ass fell asleep and I couldn't move my legs. When I tried to shake them awake, I nearly lost my footing. I managed to crawl down to safety just before unintentionally somersaulting over the rocks.

"I'd like to cancel my stand-up paddleboard tour," I requested. I'd signed up for the class the day before, not wanting time on my hands.

The resort manager at the front desk stared blankly. She was covered in tattoos and strategically placed face piercings. "May I ask why you want to cancel?"

"I overheard guests talking about a dead body in the water. It seems unsanitary."

"A dead body? Could you wait a moment?" She disappeared through a door behind the desk and returned moments later.

"No," she giggled, "he was drunk and passed out."

I stared at the red lotus tattoo carved down her right forearm. I didn't think she was being very compassionate.

"Look," I said through gritted teeth, "I'm not going. What about the Breakthrough Breathwork class?" I didn't know what it was, but it sounded like something I'd benefit from.

"Oh, that's no longer being offered," she sighed.

I didn't bother Melissa with any of it. She had a hundred classes to teach during the day, and she wasn't responsible for fixing my foul humor. I meandered back to the cabana, where I sulked for the whole afternoon. The dark cloud of spite and bitterness was back and spooning me in bed. *What am I doing here?* While Melissa and the others on the retreat saluted the sun and *om*'d, I was ohmygodding and counting the hours until I could go home.

The day before I headed back to New York, Melissa convinced me to join her and twenty others in a sacred ritual called a temazcal. A female shaman, dressed in a colorful cape and a simple headband of feathers, met us in front of a frighteningly small igloo-like structure. My guess was it was meant to symbolize Mother Earth's womb.

"The focus," Ms. Shaman purred, "is on an area of your life that needs improving." I leaned into Melissa beside me and whispered, "We don't have that kind of time." Jokes aside, I thought the experience might release me from my emotional shackles, and I might emerge anew. Maybe I'd stop saying "emotional shackles."

We kissed the ground before entering, out of respect, like knocking before entering a room or, in this case, a womb. Once inside, I knelt with the others, sitting shoulder to shoulder, watching a man place volcanic stones in a shallow pit in the center of the igloo. Ms. Shaman asked us to shout, "La puerta!" The man closed the makeshift door and covered the hole in the ceiling with thick blankets. "Remember, you can leave at any time."

I looked around the dark and moist womb and thought, *Huh, just like I remember it.*

Ms. Shaman poured water on the hot stones, releasing steam into the air and turning the heat up. I wondered how hot it would get. April in Cambodia hot? *The Towering Inferno* hot? I was all for flushing out toxins and whatnot, but I was concerned the steam was singeing my eyebrows.

We chanted, introduced ourselves, and shared our reasons for joining the ceremony. My wombmates were vulnerable and sincere. They confessed to family conflicts, professional setbacks, and a few sick and dying pets. I was the character Morales from *A Chorus Line*. I felt nothing.

Instead, I flashed back to an acting class I took in my teens. Our teacher divided the class into two rows and had us kneel on the floor and raise our arms, clasping the hands of the person across from us. One by one, we entered the tunnel. Those on the outside dropped their arms and squeezed, making it difficult to crawl through—thus re-creating the birth canal. When it was my turn, I'd stopped midway in a fit of laughter and got caught in the canal.

When Ms. Shaman called on me, I said something about letting go of the past. It was insincere. And the laugh was right there on the surface, waiting. Thankfully, I was able to squash it.

After what felt like an hour but was only ten minutes, the group slowly emerged from the igloo. I craved a cold shower and an oxygen tank. We still had three more rounds to go.

Back inside for the final round, I lay my head on Mother Earth's lap, which was colder and less disorienting than sitting upright and cross-legged, like I was during the first three rounds. Ms. Shaman asked us to express our wishes for humanity using one word. I thought, *Great! One word. We'll be out of here in no time.* The group started.

"Love."

"Kindness."

"Grace."

When it was my turn, I uttered the first thing that popped into my head: "Help."

It was ironic because I was too shut down to receive any kind of help—from my wombmates or anyone else. Mexico was supposed to be this courageous show of independence, defiance, and proof that I was over Julian. Unfortunately, it didn't work out that way.

It wasn't long before those after me turned one word into short stories and news reports. *You're not following directions. Shut up about the pending extinction of the Iberian lynx and let me out!*

When I got back home to New York, I resumed my rightful place under the coffee table in my apartment. I'd underestimated revenge travel. I hadn't anticipated how deeply emotional and unhappy I was. Wow, settling an imaginary score had some real negative and demoralizing consequences. Still, I couldn't let Julian think that I was left behind and wallowing.

Over Labor Day weekend, Nicole and I strolled through Central Park. We stopped at Bethesda Terrace, sat at the fountain's edge, and people-watched. "Hey, what are you doing for your birthday?" she asked. It was coming up in a few weeks and would be my first birthday since the breakup.

"No plans yet."

"I can't believe my dad's going to Paris with her," Nicole said, jealous.

"Really? When?" No good was going to come from Nicole's answer. But I stuck my hand in the fire anyway.

"Actually, around your birthday."

It was strategically timed. Julian was taunting me. "Looky here, ye outdated girlfriend. See me in my beret and loafers (no socks) sitting in the Air France lounge, polishing off a baguette with an absinthe chaser before boarding my flight to Charles de Gaulle without you."

He dared me to get off the floor—again.

My thirst for justice strengthened. I had to find a place to go for my birthday. But where, and do what? And then, like manna from heaven, I got an email from a credit card company with an unbelievable deal: five days and nights at Sun Stars Resort in Turks and Caicos, including airfare, ground transportation to and from the hotel, three meals a day, and an unlimited open bar. Like I was going to pass up an offer like that? I couldn't point out Turks and Caicos on a map, but it didn't matter. Like the yoga retreat in Mexico, matching my ex, frequent flyer mile for frequent flyer mile, was all the motivation I needed.

Accepting offers solely because they seemed like good bargains wasn't new to me.

I'd received one of those Valpak coupons in the mail when I was living in Los Angeles. The arch of my right foot had been throbbing for days, and I hadn't found a new podiatrist after my old one retired. Nothing says old Jew like a podiatrist. And then, bam! Valpak arrived. Inside was a coupon for a complimentary consultation with a podiatrist in Van Nuys—along with offers for a free sealer wax at Jiffy Lube and 40 percent off braces at Gentle Dental.

During the exam, the doctor asked me to walk down a long hallway so he could analyze my gait—I'm assuming. When the exam was over, he suggested surgery to remove both of my bunions. But I only had one, and it was on my left foot. It could've been worse. I could've redeemed the offer for liposuction at the Supercuts on Wilshire.

But a deal is a deal. Sun Stars Resort, Turks and Caicos, here I come—wherever you are.

Between twenty-eight thousand and thirty thousand feet over the Atlantic Ocean, Guy Fieri's doppelgänger and his wife stood in the aisle next to me. Standing in the aisles while the plane is in the air is like standing up in a rowboat and rocking it from side to side. It makes me nuts. Then, they changed out of their flannel ensemble into a floral sarong for her and board shorts for him. It was like Guy and his bride gave the go-ahead, because travelers on all sides started shedding their city clothes for tropical island wear. *Keep your clothes on. This isn't a department store dressing room.* I kept my clothes on—clothes that screamed, "A winter storm is coming."

The drink cart rolled by, and it looked like everyone on the plane stocked up on wine and beer. The festivities and raucous behavior continued. I wondered if the plane would be making a quick turnaround after landing at Providenciales Airport and heading back to New York, because I already wanted to go home. An announcement came on the PA. "Please store your tray tables and prepare for landing." I tried to silence my doubts. *I'm not going to let these people dump on my experience. A beautiful resort and spa are waiting for me.*

As it turned out, the hotel shuttle wasn't just for me, like I'd thought. Anyone checking into any hotel on the island (islands?) could hop on. It was standing room only. And I was lucky to snag a seat. It was like a rolling party bus of overaged frat boys and the casts from every city in the *Housewives* franchise. I sat next to half-naked, rowdy adults chanting, "Freedom!" and fist-bumping anyone within reach. I hugged the window with my face. *Have you never seen sand? Palm trees? A shuttle bus?* If this was a preview of things to come, then I was in serious trouble. I had hoped for a mellow place to indulge in some pampering. How was it possible to feel worse than when I'd boarded the plane in New York? Guy and his wife cackled behind me, and I swear, I could taste their alcohol breath in my mouth.

The hotel lobby opened onto the Atlantic Ocean. Okay, that was special. At least the place was charming. White-gloved attendants circulated nearby, carrying trays of glasses filled with orange liquid. "Would you care for one? It's the hotel's specialty."

I downed it in a single swallow. "Oh," I said, choking, "that's alcohol!"

"Yes," he said with a snort, "that's the special part."

I was behaving like an Amish teen on her Rumspringa, tasting the modern world for the first time.

My room was functional and lovely. For some travelers, luxury is a plush hotel bathrobe and furry slippers. For others, it's a poolside butler and a champagne vending machine. For me, it's an in-room coffee maker. I like to control my caffeine intake—when, where, and frequency. One look at the single-cup Nespresso machine, and I forgot all about Guy and the flying fraternity.

At eight o'clock the following morning, I put on my bathing suit, had a cup of coffee, and headed to the hotel café for breakfast. Everywhere I looked along the way, couples were lounging by the saltwater pool, strolling along the beach, and making hearts in the sand with their toes. And everyone was sipping the resort's specialty drink. It looked like a television commercial for Sandals. I had the sneaking suspicion that, like Sandals, Sun Stars was for couples only—engaged, honeymooning, or parents running away from their kids.

For the record, I never saw Sun Stars advertised as a couples' resort. On the other hand, I didn't exactly do a deep dive. The more I thought about it, the more I realized I didn't see anyone who looked like me on the airplane or the shuttle. By which I mean *solamente*. It would appear that I missed this little nugget of information.

The café hostess seated me at a table for two, took my order, and removed the extra table setting. Her assumption was insulting. I felt the eyes of twenty or more couples around me staring and pitying. So, to feel more confident, I pretended my lover had the runs because of a contaminated lettuce leaf and was taking care of business in our honeymoon suite.

After that first meal, and for the remainder of the trip, I swiped enough food at breakfast so I could eat lunch and dinner in my room. Usually, I'm okay eating alone in a restaurant. But I felt pressured to have a good time, and I was significantly more insecure thanks to the breakup.

I'd unknowingly gone to a couples' resort where alcohol, romance, and sex were on the menu and all around me. To avoid all that, I chose to squirrel away hard-boiled eggs, fruit, yogurt, and what added up to be several loaves of bread, like a senior citizen on a fixed income. The truth was, I didn't have much of an appetite. Mourning my philandering ex was a very effective appetite suppressor.

I carried my knapsack of groceries out of the café and walked to the spa. I'd signed up for a reflexology session. Sometimes, someone touching my feet is more relaxing than a full-body massage. I was led into a room by a handsome masseur with intense gray eyes. They looked like they were made of glass. I lay on the table, and he dimmed the lights. He uttered a few mantras and then was quiet, leaving me to enjoy the soft sounds of pan flutes and wind chimes.

My muscles eased within the first few minutes, and my body began to untangle—slowly and gratefully. My long breaths and deep sighs were audible and involuntary. Whatever gunk I was clinging to, my healer seemed to release it through my heels and soles.

But then, as if taking out a personal vendetta, the masseur started digging his nails into the tops of my feet. It was aggressive. How could he not feel my skin underneath his nails? A warm sensation ran down my left middle toe. *Did he just draw blood?*

"Can you please go easy with your nails?" I asked.

He stared at me, searing into my soul with his glass lasers. Those lasers were screaming, "I'm barely touching you. If I were stabbing you, you'd know it."

He didn't apologize or pull back on the pressure. So I got up abruptly and left. Maybe he didn't understand English.

I wasn't hankering for the beach, but that's where my feet took me. Had my mind led the charge, I would've been in my hotel room making coffee.

Several people were playing volleyball a few feet from where I settled to read under a tree. Come on, volleyball? Volleyball was Julian's game of choice. Even in his absence, he was present.

"Hey, would you like to play?" a sweet voice asked.

"Me?" I looked up. A freckled and shapely young woman wearing a tankini stood smiling at me.

"Yeah. Do you play? My friend Rebecca needs a break."

"Uh, well, I'm not very good, or even slightly good. But okay."

The one time Julian agreed to play with me, he gave up after ten minutes. I'd done a demi-plié to gain momentum before I served and may have added a twirl. I thought it was funny. Julian didn't. I wish I'd told him to chill out and asked him, where was the playful guy that I fell in love with? I was on his beach in the sun, which I hated, smacking a fucking ball over a fucking net with my fucking wrist because I loved him, not because I actually wanted to.

I felt gawky and stupid, frolicking with people half my age. It was the Grand Tetons of clichés. My ex's deception wasn't half as humiliating as becoming a cliché. I'd always thought I was different. But goddamn it, I was just another Stella trying to get her groove back.

After one game, Rebecca hopped up from her blanket. I'm sure replacing me so quickly had nothing to do with the fact that I couldn't see the volleyball and my team was getting hammered. I'd forgotten to put my contact lenses in.

The beach attendant never offered me a refreshing ice towel like he did for Rebecca and her wrinkle-free friends. I felt invisible. I'd heard about this sort of thing happening to women of a certain age. I'd read articles and listened to the complaints. But surely, it didn't apply to me. How could it?

I never paid much attention to getting older or the emotional and physical by-products when I was with Julian. Maybe it was because I always saw myself through his eyes—only adoration and desire.

Since no one was paying attention to me, I removed a stand-up paddleboard and a paddle from the activity rack on the beach. I did not ask for permission; nor did I sign them out.

Take that, Sun Stars.

I walked the board into the ocean with more than a little trepidation. I'm afraid of large bodies of water if I don't know what's swimming around my ankles. I was relieved to see the ocean floor beneath me. I knelt on my board, and when I felt balanced, I kicked my legs up and stood on my head. No one noticed. Yes, I expected a reaction from the couples splashing nearby and the throuple looking for seashells. I was in a DayGlo bikini, for crying out loud. Now that's invisible.

Not much changed in how I spent the next three days. I swiped food, ate alone, read, and gazed at my navel. And then it was my birthday. I was in my hotel room making my third cup of coffee when there was a knock at the door. I couldn't imagine who it could be. I hadn't ordered room service. For half a second, I thought maybe Julian had spoken to Nicole and found out where I was. He'd taken a break from stuffing his girlfriend's face with Camembert while sailing on a Bateaux Mouches, called my hotel, and sent something. Despite what happened, some part of me wanted this to be true. In the rom-com version, Julian is on his knees outside my door and, in perfect French, begs for forgiveness. S'il te plait, pardonne-moi. Je suis un con et un imbécile.

I looked through the peephole and opened the door. A staff member, wearing a white chef's coat, held a silver tray with one slice of chocolate cake on a plate. "Happy Birthday" was written in white frosting along the rim. How did the hotel know? And then I remembered, I'd told the reservation operator it was my birthday so I might get a room upgrade.

Cake Man placed the tray on a table in the entryway and studied the room. "Oh, no one else is here?"

Seriously? It was so intrusive. How did he know that my lover wasn't still shitting his brains out in the bathroom?

"Nope, just me."

Cake Man turned and walked out, shaking his head like he was disappointed. Take a number, dude.

The couples' resort was a bad idea. I get it—now! What did I expect from coupons, couples, and trying to keep up with my ex? What did I think was going to happen? But that's just it: I didn't think. I was on some kind of autopilot. My only objective was to keep moving. And if I was lucky, maybe, just maybe, I'd outrun the pain and eventually forget Julian altogether.

————

Several weeks passed, and I was in my apartment watching an episode of *The Golden Girls*, tap dancing along with Blanche and Rose. I played my feet like an instrument, step-ball-changing and flapping. The sound of metal on my hardwood living room floor always puts me in a good mood. Although, I can't say what my downstairs neighbors thought.

Revenge travel was a bust. No one, including my ex, knew that I was playing this game. And he certainly wouldn't feel my wrath or anything else as it pertained to me. I placed the back of my right hand against my forehead in a melodramatic repose. "I'll never love again. I'll never love traveling again. I'm through, I'm through— with all of it." And then my phone rang. It was Nicole.

"You'll never guess where my dad just got back from."

When we finished talking, I hung up. And then I dialed. "Hello, Icelandair. I'd like to make a reservation."

Before you come at me, let me explain. Julian and I had talked about going to Iceland ever since I told him my ex-husband had gone to see a David Bowie concert in Reykjavík. Iceland was mine!

My righteous outrage ratcheted up, and my self-respect went AWOL. I was obsessed, so very obsessed, and I would get my revenge. Julian may have gone to Iceland first, but I'd make sure I had a *much* better time. I'd draw the line at eating horsemeat, but everything else was fair game.

A month later, I checked into my hotel in Reykjavík, unpacked, and strolled around downtown. It was ten o'clock in the evening, but it looked like one in the afternoon. It's disorienting to want to floss and sleep when people are meeting for brunch under your hotel window. Nothing would make me happier than to tell you about the architecture or the healthy and outdoorsy-looking locals in their yummy sweaters (the city was a Patagonia catalog), but I can't. I was still numb. I was basically sleepwalking up and down Laugavegur and Bankastræti Streets, detached from my surroundings. I noticed very little. Reykjavík was more like a waystation, a place to sleep at the end of my daily excursions.

For the next four days, I took different Gray Line shuttles each morning and toured various parts of Iceland. After breakfast on my first full day in the land of ice and fire, I climbed onto the bus, heading to a stable to go horseback riding. I faced a group of strangers staring at me. But, unlike in the café at Sun Stars, I stared confidently back, and my insecurity and Greta Garbo–like "I vant to be alone" energy vanished. I sat in the first available seat and introduced myself to my seatmate. And I didn't stop talking until we reached the horse stables. I loved Iceland! It was so unexpected—it'd been a minute since I loved anything, and the feeling was a shock to my system. Maybe the fresh air had extra oxygen and I was releasing more serotonin.

The horses in Iceland are much smaller than those in North America and are surprisingly gentle. Several nuzzled against each other in an open field. They behaved more like golden retrievers than horses. While a female wrangler helped me choose a horse, she told me she was originally from New York. She'd moved to Iceland and almost immediately met a man, who was now her fiancé.

"I'd never go back," she said as she prepared my saddle.

"Maybe I should stay and get me one of those," I offered, climbing onto the horse.

"Yeah, they're just giving them away."

I trotted toward the others in my group, looked back, and shared a laugh with my wrangler. I'd forgotten how good laughing felt.

The ride was a walk on flat terrain, with stops every few feet to readjust someone's loose stirrup. After an hour of this and nearly being lulled to sleep by my gentle steed, we were back at the stable. It may not have been the thrill that I was seeking, but I wasn't on a beach, and I was happy.

When I went to bed that night, the dark cloud I'd been living under lifted. It was a miracle. My chest didn't feel as heavy, and I couldn't wait for the morning. The anticipation of descending into the throat of a dormant volcano made me giddy.

Oskar, a man in his sixties, was our driver and tour guide for the day. He greeted me at my hotel with an enthusiastic, double-handed wave. After the thirty-minute drive, he parked the bus in a clearing beneath the Blue Mountains. They gave the surrounding area a surreal and otherworldly appearance. The howling wind, intermittent drizzle, and mild temperature were ideal conditions for the two-mile hike to the geological site. Oskar pointed to the singular path, and I started off. I had to move. Every step forward felt like I was leaving more of my past behind. I couldn't wait for my fellow passengers to get their jackets on and tie their shoes. My future was waiting!

After a moderate trek, we arrived at the rickety platform at the entrance to the volcano, where a couple of guides were waiting for us. They outfitted our small group of eight with helmets, head-lamps, and harnesses. Some of my new friends chose not to take the six-minute drop and waited off to the side. It was four hundred feet to the bottom of the crater in an open cable lift. My sudden excite-ment reminded me of my old self. I rushed through the crowd, nearly knocking down Marvin, an older gentleman using a cane.

Four of us stepped inside the metal cage. We hooked a chain attached to the railing through the front of our harnesses for safety. As we dropped into the bowels of the volcano, I grinned. The natu-ral light faded. Our headlamps provided the only light source when we hit the rock floor. The interior, a once-blazing abyss, was quiet and still. The yellows, reds, and black colors on the walls and floor looked like an elephant's drawing of hell.

I asked one of my new friends if they would take my picture. Taking photographs is one of the drawbacks of traveling alone when a selfie just won't cut it. And my selfie skills are appalling. I always come out looking like a potato.

Much of the time, when Julian and I traveled, we went where he wanted to go. We ate our way through Madrid when I would've pre-ferred walking the Camino de Santiago. I watched him play poker in Majorca instead of biking through Scotland. And when we went skiing in Quebec, I would've rather tracked gorillas in Uganda. But I didn't mind. Being together was all that mattered to me. And after a while, at some point when I wasn't looking, I'd let go of my wants and priorities and I'd become a shadow of myself. But now, I could be the intrepid traveler I saw myself to be.

The next stop was Reynisfjara, the world-famous nontropical beach of black sand.

"Be careful near the ocean's edge," Oskar admonished. The beach's beauty was haunting, with its imposing basalt columns, often called organ pipes. They rose on one side, and the roaring waves Oskar was warning us about crashed on the other. "It can be dangerous," he continued. "You can be swept out to sea. Many lives, mainly Chinese people, have been lost because they turned their backs to the water." I don't know why he singled out the Chinese, as any nationality could be guilty of turning their backs.

Throughout the day, Oskar took every opportunity to share vivid Icelandic folklore about trolls and tragic stories of death and destruction. Given the abundance of crosses and cemeteries we passed, he had plenty of chances and just as many tales. And when he ran out of ghosts and elves, he asked if anyone was interested in visiting chess grandmaster Bobby Fischer's gravesite. Crickets.

A new driver and tour guide arrived at my hotel the following morning. He was a sexy Icelander named Skarpi with a dimpled chin and a musical Icelandic accent. I had to stop myself from calling him Sharpie. I sat in the front passenger seat because the bus was packed. Skarpi and I flirted the entire hour-and-a-half ride to the Langjökull Glacier. At least, I think it was flirting. We made eye contact, and I complimented him on his driving. And when he talked, I leaned in close to listen. At one point, I playfully punched his arm like we were kindergarteners teasing one another on the playground. Skarpi was the first man I'd been attracted to since Julian. I was remarkably out of practice.

Skarpi and I were so deep in conversation that I forgot we weren't alone.

Someone in the group asked him about his family, interrupting our discussion about his professional basketball career. I bristled.

What a busybody. He talked about his kids—three, with one on the way—and then told everyone he'd recently researched vasectomies on the internet. Had it not been for his family, we might've had a promising future together. "I live near the president of Iceland, Guðni Thorlacius Jóhannesson," Skarpi said, changing the subject. "And the singer Björk."

"Try saying your president's name ten times fast," I said. My confidence blossomed sitting on a plush gray leather seat beside Skarpi, barreling down Road 550. "And I love Björk's song 'Human Behaviour.'" I was shameless.

"My kids walked around our neighborhood," Skarpi continued, "collecting bottles and cans, raising money for a school project. When they reached the president's house, he and his wife, who's Jewish, . . ."

I prayed Skarpi wouldn't offer a trope like, "You know how Jewish people love their seltzer."

". . . they told my kids they didn't have any bottles or cans because . . ."

I held my breath.

". . . neither he nor his wife drink soda."

I exhaled. Skarpi's seductive accent made up for his long and boring story, which sounded rehearsed.

I was concerned about leaving an exhaust-filled carbon footprint if I snowmobiled on the Langjökull Glacier. I wanted reassurance that my ride wouldn't have a catastrophic climatic outcome and word of it wouldn't get back to Greta Thunberg. I asked Gunnar, who was outfitting me with snow pants and thick black gloves, what he thought.

"It's so enormous," he said in perfect English, handing me my boots. "I'm not too concerned." Didn't people say this about

Antarctica not too long ago? I climbed onto my snowmobile, revved the machine, and peeled out.

Thirty minutes in, we stopped for a photo op. I stood on my snowmobile and asked my new friend Susan to take my picture. I couldn't resist the backdrop—tall, snowy mountain ranges and ice-filled craters. Mother Nature put in overtime here for sure. And even better, I genuinely appreciated her hard work—unlike back in Mexico.

Skarpi approached and asked if I would mind taking a young Iranian boy in our group on the back of my snowmobile for the rest of the tour. The child had been on his brother's, and they'd crashed. Everyone was okay, but the machine was undrivable. I wondered why he needed to tell me that the boy was Iranian.

"Of course," I replied. *Anything for you.* I hoped that I wasn't drooling.

I thought it was odd that the child's parents didn't want to shake my hand, see my driver's license, or at the very least, have me sign a waiver. They were on their vehicle in the distance, and when I caught their eye, they just smiled. I was driving off with their son, with no guarantees that I'd return him. The young boy, whose name I immediately forgot (because my mind is a sieve), hopped on the back. We sped up and down the snowy slopes and took hairpin turns at forty miles an hour. I kept my passenger laughing the entire time. The optics couldn't be ignored—given a chance, I alone could mend U.S.-Iranian relations.

At every stop on the tours, I was first. The first person off the bus to witness spewing geysers, the first to walk behind the Seljalandsfoss waterfall, and the first to drink glacier water while balancing on ice axes in a plank position. Oh, how I'd missed myself. Before long, I was seeking out couples in love and offering to take *their* picture.

I'd spent a week adventuring in the world's most isolated and exquisite landscapes. I didn't know if it was me or a geyser erupting in the distance, but I was vibrating. The gap between the person I was and the person who'd emerged in Iceland was closing.

Revenge travel didn't miraculously put an end to my wretched heartache or fulfill my fantasy of getting back at my ex. What it did do in Iceland was restore my joy of traveling on *my* terms, with only *my* desires to satisfy. The sweetest revenge, I decided, would be when I forgot about my ex entirely. And to do that, I had to sit still and stop smothering my sadness with hotel reservations.

In time, that's exactly what happened. My middle finger joined the other fingers, and revenge travel was permanently grounded.

nine

Between Fantasy and Reality Is a Stripper Pole

THE SUREST WAY TO PUT ME on the defensive is to tell me I can't do something. People love to impose their limitations onto others—as if we're all the same, with the same skill sets and talents. They also love to make assumptions about what's possible or no longer possible, especially when we hit a certain age. Maybe I don't have any limitations. I don't know what I'm capable of; nor do these idiots. Their meritless notions are a gauntlet thrown at my feet. And now I have to drag myself out of bed and defend myself.

This defiance is the "how" and "why" that led to me standing half naked on a stage in lower Manhattan at a pole fitness competition in my late forties. A few months earlier, I'd read a cloying article about diminishing dreams and estrogen levels, and I wanted to spit. Paragraph after paragraph, the author babbled on about youthful dreams in the rearview mirror and the importance of radical acceptance. And to love my crepey elbows. "This is life," I read. "The beauty of age is knowing when to let go of activities no longer viable." The article concluded with, "Embrace this stage of life. Think of your sagging earlobes as signs of maturity and wisdom."

I immediately signed up for a pole class. Because now, I had something to prove.

Ironically, I'd had a run-in with the pole fifteen years earlier.

I was living in Los Angeles, and one day I saw an ad for a new kind of fitness class: Introduction to the Stripper Pole. I signed up because I was curious and thought people would think I was audacious. It was pretty risqué at the time.

Maggie Lord was the owner of You Foxy Studios. She'd turned pole dancing into a workout, branding herself the Pole Healer. It got so popular that poles started popping up in bedrooms and corporate offices from coast to coast. Women took control of their sexuality and empowered themselves, blah, blah, blah—I mean, great for them, but what I really cared about was that Maggie's husband was a producer on the television show *The X Files*. It came up on the website when I researched her class. I was convinced he'd put me on the show if I could just meet him.

My plan went something like this: I'd befriend Maggie in class. She'd invite me over for some holiday or a Hollywood who's who confab. She'd introduce me to her husband, and after the initial pleasantries, I'd ask to use the bathroom and then pretend to be lost so I could snoop around. I'd find Mr. Producer's study, where television scripts are stacked on a coffee table. I'd place my headshot and resume on top—a serious performer never leaves home without them. Shortly afterward, I'd receive a call from *The X Files'* casting director offering me a recurring role playing a terrorist in a coma.

Sadly, Maggie's class wasn't for me, and we didn't become friends. It was too kooky—too much "pleasure journey" and "erotic truth" talk. When I explore my body, which the class was encouraged to do, I prefer doing so in the privacy of my bedroom and not with a bunch of strangers writhing on their bellies in a dimly lit studio.

But after reading that stupid article, it was intolerable to think that climbing a pole was behind me. I wanted to see for myself and not be swayed by my naked reflection goading me in the full-length mirror in my bedroom.

My instructor at Fitness and Pole in Midtown, Holly, was a tall woman with a jet-black mullet, biceps for days, and zero percent body fat. My washed-out bird tattoo on my ankle looked weak compared to her red-inked MOM across her chest. From the first class, it was a lovefest between the chrome pole and me. I can't say why exactly, but straddling and squeezing a metal rod between my legs agreed with me. I was all in. I bought booty shorts from the studio's retail shop and non-slide liquid to give me a tackier grip. I made friends with burlesque dancers and trapeze performers. Boy, did I regret not running away from home and joining the circus when I had the chance.

Only a month after I'd started, Holly told our class that the U.S. National Pole Championship was coming to New York. She encouraged everyone to participate, even us beginners. What better way to shut the naysayers up than signing up for a competition? In private, I asked Holly if she thought I was ready. Two days earlier, I was cleared to join Level 2. But I'd only hung upside down a handful of times.

"Definitely," Holly said. "There's an over-forty category." I didn't remember telling her my age. What, I wondered, could've possibly given me away? Her assumption only fueled the "I'll show you" fire building inside me.

When I returned to my apartment, in a rush of emboldened confidence I registered for the competition. I didn't overthink, over-analyze, or ask for anyone's opinion. And then, I made the mistake of watching videos of past competitions on YouTube. Watching participants fly around the spinning poles made me dizzy. I'd never be able to spin. I get nauseous reading road signs when I'm sitting in the passenger seat of a car. Women defied gravity and contorted their bodies in ways I never imagined were anatomically possible. And they did it while wearing what amounted to a loin cloth on the bottom and a headband strapped across their boobs. One woman went into a vertical split against the pole, holding on by the back of her kneecap.

I bought a pole for my apartment so I could practice every day. It stood at the intersection of the bathroom and the kitchen. Occasionally, my foot would get caught on the edge of the sink, but I persevered. Funnily enough, when building maintenance came to fix my toilet one day, the man walked around the pole like it was a support column and part of the architecture. As much as I enjoy believing that I'm unique in all ways, I thought there had to be at least one other poler in the building of five hundred apartments—and that's why the maintenance man didn't bat an eye.

I began training like a professional athlete. I've never trained for a competition that demanded I be physically fit, like a marathon, bodybuilding, or a beauty pageant. I've dieted and been in musicals. And while both took discipline, neither required muscular grip strength or the ability to climb using my armpits.

I didn't know what music to use for my routine. I'd been listening to a lot of Sade and chose the song "Your Love Is King"—a soulful and jazzy vocal. It was slow and controlled, like I hoped to be on the pole. My friend Sharon, who played Victoria the White Cat in the national touring company of *Cats* (and never lets me forget it), helped me choreograph a two-and-a-half-minute routine.

I walked across town several times a week for classes and private sessions with Holly. She was a four-time champion. I wasn't going to train with some slacker. I pulled out all the stops and spared no expense. My self-respect and ego were on the line. In addition to giving me feedback on my routine, Holly told me to avoid salty foods so I wouldn't retain water. And to consider an enema on show day.

After three months of preparation, my inner thighs were black and blue, my calves were swollen and veiny, and the tops of my feet were torn like they'd been repeatedly whacked with a steel pipe. I was ready.

At six in the morning on the day of the competition, I put on my costume—a black bra with strategic cutouts and teeny tiny black shorts—underneath my street clothes. I'd chosen to accessorize with red ropes that crisscrossed the length of my forearms, which I threw into my backpack to put on later. And I would perform barefoot. My bunion and recently fallen arches prevented me from wearing spiky high heels. I'm afraid it's orthotics and cushioned soles from now on. Getting older is fun—and sexy.

I rode my bicycle to the theater while drizzling rain fell on my freshly flat-ironed hair. I was nervous for the first time since I embarked on my pole journey. And I questioned why my rebel yell had to be such a big production number. I'll tell you why—because my motto has always been, "Go big or don't bother." As uber model Linda Evangelista once quipped, "We have this saying, Christy

[Turlington] and I . . . we don't wake up for less than $10,000 a day." Same. Only instead of money, it's someone challenging my ability and fearing they might be right about me.

Nerves aside, I'd picked up the gauntlet, and I wouldn't turn back. I'd told too many people about my courageous quest. I'd be embarrassed if I didn't see it through. Arriving at the competition venue in lower Manhattan, I dismounted my bike and locked it to a tree.

My performance was going to be for women like me everywhere. What I was about to do was worthy of *CNN Hero of the Year.* "Thank you, Anderson. What an honor. My mission is more important than saving lives or teaching pigs to paint. I'm speaking to women everywhere—dimpled knees, hairy toes, and dry toast-like vagina aside—and letting them know that anything is possible. For every woman who's ever been told, 'You can't'; 'Your bones are brittle'; 'You're an idiot,' this award is for you. If you can dream it, you can be it."

The welcome desk and the lobby were abuzz with competitors. I was thrilled to be a part of the pole community. Men and women wearing leg warmers and not much else kicked, bent, and twisted, warming up on the hideous red carpet in the hallway and arching over railings and chairs.

But walking up the three flights to the dressing room, I grew increasingly self-conscious. *This is ridiculous. I'm ridiculous.* I didn't owe women everywhere anything. Unlike when I did stand-up comedy and could hide behind jokes and self-deprecating humor, the pole was too narrow to hide anything. My crepey elbows and flawed arrogance were about to be exposed.

Mismatched chairs and chipped mirrors were strewn around

the dressing room. A female stage manager, wearing a headset and holding a clipboard, entered. "You have a half hour to practice," she barked. "Please head to the stage." I didn't know that we'd have a chance to rehearse our routines before the competition—and in front of everyone. I felt sick.

Two poles were set up on the stage—one static and one spin. They looked much taller than the one I had suctioned to the eight-foot ceiling in my apartment. I stood in line, bare shoulder to nearly bare shoulder, with the fittest-looking bodies I'd ever seen, waiting for my turn. I wondered which of these contortionists and acrobats were in my group of forty-ites. I wanted to size up my competition.

After watching a few very flexible athletes, I had to admit that my righteous anger had overestimated my skill set. Oh, I can sure talk a good game. Is there a medal for the most convincing imposter? When I was young, I tried convincing New Yorkers that I was a ballet dancer by waddling around like a duck. And now my hip dislocates when I fart. I was in way over my head—and if I wasn't careful, I just might land on it.

When it was my turn, I attached some old headphones to my iPod Nano and clipped it to my shirt. I took my opening position, leaning back against the static pole, with fifty pairs of eyes watching. To my right, a young woman spun and twirled, hair whipping around her face. She's going to have a pinched nerve or bone spurs in her neck when she's my age, for sure.

I walked offstage when I was through, relieved the rehearsal was over. I was about to return to the dressing room and "an actor prepares," but no one else was leaving. I looked at the wall clock. Damn, there was still time for another practice run. I didn't want to run it again. I wanted to have an excuse. If I gave a shitty performance, I could say, "I might've done better if only I had more time to practice." Wasn't my presence here proof enough that I'd succeeded?

Letting myself off the hook with excuses was just like me. Like when I'd said going to theater school for college was a waste of time. Better that I learn medieval history and elementary statistics than risk failure at the one thing I was truly passionate about.

But something about this time was different, and I got back on stage. No fallback or lies to tell myself. Uh-oh. Was this a sign of age and wisdom?

An hour later, back in the dressing room an announcement came over the PA system that the Masters (over-forty) group was up next. I tightened the ropes on my forearms, applied another layer of Vaseline to my lips, and walked backstage.

Showtime.

I stood in the wings, waiting for my cue. I told myself that it didn't matter what might happen—falling, tripping, or sliding down the pole face first. I'd already won.

The stage manager gave me the signal, and I walked out on stage with my head held high. It was so quiet in the audience, I could hear people thinking, "She obviously thinks she's got something to prove."

Sade started singing, and I pressed my back against the pole. My routine started with a couple of seductive body rolls with my bare midsection. After a few other minor moves, I started my ascent. When I climbed to the top, I performed my favorite trick—the crossed-ankle sit. From there, I twisted my lower body to one side, spiraling myself around the pole for a few rotations, and then dropped to the floor in painfully slow motion. *Do not fall* rang in my ears. I checked out for a few crucial moments, forgot the choreography, and had to improvise. In another spot, I rushed and got ahead of the music. But it's all about how you finish. And I hit my final pose, coiled around the base of the pole, with my hair loosely draped over my shoulders. I couldn't stop grinning. When I heard hands clapping, I almost started laughing. My body shook with delirium and relief. I sprang up from the floor, bowed, and skipped off stage, self-satisfied.

When I passed the stage manager, who was prepping the next competitor, she whispered, "Keep doing this."

What? I thought. *Wow, I must have really slayed out there.*

I sprinted to the dressing room, taking the stairs two at a time. Oh my gosh, I felt so proud and cocky. While I got dressed, I couldn't help thinking about what might have been had I stuck with the Pole Healer fifteen years earlier. Had I continued, I might've had both a television career and a pole career.

When every category was finished, all of the participants gathered on stage for the awards ceremony. The host read from her index cards. "The second-place medal in the U.S National Pole Championships over-forty group is . . ." I thought I'd misheard when my name was called. It was truly unexpected and absurd but also so right.

The host placed a silver medal around my neck, just like at the Olympics. The thunderous applause that I imagined was deafening. I also imagined grabbing the microphone and thanking my agent, my parents, and the man upstairs.

As I pedaled back to my apartment, I couldn't stop thinking about the stage manager's encouraging words. The little attention she'd offered me was a formidable invitation. *She must be right!*

I should keep doing this. It's almost Pavlovian. Maybe it was the authority and the power of her headset. Or the award confirming what I'd been yelling about all along—"It's not too late until I say it is!" My mind was made up. I was going pro. If I could place second after only three months of training, imagine what I could accomplish after four or five months. Pole World Champion. The Pole Masters Cup. Not to mention speaking engagements, conventions, and branding my own line of travel poles and knee pads.

The adrenaline was still pumping when I hung up my bicycle in my apartment. I poured myself a shot of tequila and sat at my kitchen table. Was I seriously going to upend my life to pursue the pole? Maybe. But I was in a writing and teaching Pilates groove—a slow groove nevertheless, which was also why the stage manager's remark was so tempting. I'm weak to anything that smells of a "quick fix" when things aren't moving fast enough—or going my way. And so I might mistake an innocent suggestion for an exit ramp. Also, I was still high from performing, so naturally, I believed that poling was the *it* I'd been looking for!

I poured myself another shot and looked at the eight-foot pole in the middle of my apartment and giggled. Becoming a pole sensation might've been an awesome pursuit back in the day. But on this day, I was forty-eight. And I've come to see that not everything I tried or was good at was telling me I had to drop what I was doing and make a sharp right. I'd worked too hard to stay in my lane and stay the course. After two more shots, I forgot about poling professionally. I'd have to be content dancing and poling alone like no one's watching.

I hadn't eaten anything all day, so I went into the kitchen. I'd probably regret it in the morning, but I microwaved a broccoli and bean burrito. I wasn't in training anymore. When I was done, I went into the bedroom to change out of my pole costume. I pulled down my booty shorts and was shocked to see that I'd been wearing them backward and inside out.

ten

Show and Tell

WHEN I WAS A SOPHOMORE in high school, I met a charismatic senior named Alan Reeves, né Adelson. Reeves was his stage name. A stage name?! I'd read about celebrities changing their names, but I'd never met anyone who had. Alan thought Reeves sounded more professional and bankable than Adelson.

Alan cast me in the Spring Finale, the end-of-year student show. He was the overall director and in charge of the entire production, from casting to program design. Working with other theater nerds and talented dorks and watching Alan's command of the stage was the highlight of the school year. I was far from an academic or an intellectual. Mostly, I thought school was boring and a waste of my time. Why bother memorizing the periodic table and learning all the verses of "America the Beautiful" when I had more pressing concerns, like managing my body image? With each passing semester, my concerns and insecurities grew—as did my nose. I wouldn't have survived high school with my self-esteem intact had it not been for theater. There's no doubt I would've graduated with an eating disorder (like the rest of my classmates did) if I hadn't had the stage as my outlet.

Alan was a living and breathing showman. He was precocious and I envied him for having parents who were stage parents who understood his dreams and fostered his talents. He sang Sinatra and Bennett and opened for legendary comedians at hotels in the Catskills. He entertained on cruise ships, which I thought was glitzy and glamorous. The only cruise ship entertainers I knew were the ones I watched on *The Love Boat*. He took the expression "mature beyond his years" to a whole new level. Finally, someone I could relate to.

Alan and I had been sneaking around and secretly seeing each other for weeks, hiding from the cast and crew. We didn't want to mix our professional and personal lives. Dating Alan meant that I was one step closer to fame—what, with all the people he knew. He'd undoubtedly help me and open some doors. Maybe I'd meet Charo or Todd Bridges.

During theater rehearsal one day, Alan took my hand and led me backstage.

"I just got a call from my manager," he said, cupping my face in his hands. "The Royal Mediterranean booked me on a two-week cruise. I leave the day after tomorrow."

"Really?" I turned away, trying to hide my disappointment. What would Alan's absence mean for the future of our relationship? And he'd miss opening night.

I turned back to him. "I mean, that's great news. It's just that I'm going to miss you."

After several beats, I exclaimed proudly, "But, the show must go on!"

And then Alan broke into a jazzy medley of "Jeepers Creepers" and "It Had to Be You"—a preview of his cruise ship act. He sang into my misty eyes. "It had to be you, wonderful you, it had to be you." Alan was Satchmo and Sinatra, all wrapped up into one gifted showman. I fell in love with that gifted showman right then and there.

The night before Alan pulled up anchor, he stopped by my parents' house to say goodbye. He gave me a journal from Fiorucci, a very happening and cool store in the '80s whose logo was two winged cherubs, heads tilted together. Alan removed his eight-by-ten black-and-white headshot that was tucked behind the last page and autographed it for me.

We walked out to the driveway, and Alan gave me a peck on the cheek. He climbed into his bronze Lincoln Continental and drove away, leaving me with the journal and my tears.

I started writing poetry that very night. It was the only way I could express my loneliness and despair. Ever since I saw *Doctor Zhivago*, I've wanted to try writing poetry. But something always held me back—I didn't have the time, inspiration, or the right kind of paper. But now my man was sailing off, and I was overflowing with emotions like that tortured soul Zhivago. The pages of blank ruled paper beckoned. And I wrote. And in late June, when Alan returned from the high seas, I wrote some more.

After Being with Him

I have no doubts now, I know how to love you and I do.
You've proved your love for me, just from your words and what
    you do.

I feel so warm and safe and oh, so good when I'm with you. I don't
ever want it to end. It feels too good. Will it always be like this,
please say yes.
My desires are stronger than they've ever been.
I want to be with you every waking minute.
I do, so want you to give me time and we shall see.

It was obvious to the trained and untrained eye that I'd never
be a Dickinson or an Eliot. Poetry was too confining, creatively. I
was too focused on rhyming because that's what I thought poetry
was. I broke my brain trying to find words that rhyme with "opus"
and "orange."

Two days after our sweet, sweet, reunion, Alan hinted at getting
back together with his former girlfriend, Kelly—a girl his own age.
He was troubled by our two-year age difference. He was leaving for
college while I would spend the summer on a teen tour. It was my
first breakup, and I was crushed and confused. And I could forget
about meeting Todd Bridges.

After a couple of days of moping and sobbing, I decided to
fight for Alan and his affection. I didn't understand anything
about relationships. But I thought I could win Alan back if I canceled my travel plans and spent the summer at home. He'd see my
commitment and kick Kelly to the curb. However, summers were
my parents' vacation—which meant no kids in the house. They'd
paid for my trip in full to ensure I'd be elsewhere for two months.
So instead, I wrote more cringe-worthy poetry while I secretly
hoped that Kelly would fall into a well, never to be seen or heard
from again. And then Alan and I would find our way back to
each other.

The teen tour was an eight-week action-packed road trip throughout the western United States—a group of fifteen- and sixteen-year-olds traveling in a deluxe Greyhound bus supervised by a few college students. There was something about riding in a motorcoach with air-conditioning and a bathroom that I found exciting. I'd never been on a bus with a bathroom. It sounded expensive and luxurious. The only people I imagined traveled this way were country singers and church groups.

At the start of the eight weeks, my parents dropped me off at JFK, kissed me goodbye, and raced out of the terminal. Their summer vacation had officially begun. I introduced myself to a few girls and made small talk while we waited to board our flight to Denver, where our bus would be waiting. These were the OG Gossip Girls. "Do you guys play any sports in school?" I asked.

No one had. I tried again. "Has anyone seen the movie *Mommie Dearest*? Faye Dunaway was so scary."

No one responded.

"I loved *Porky's*," said a girl wearing gold ballet-slipper-like shoes and bright orange leg warmers. "Have you seen it?" she asked me.

I hadn't.

But also, ballet slipper street shoes and leg warmers? There were rules. You don't wear leg warmers as an accessory. I didn't want to judge or make any assumptions, but unless she leapt onto the plane and relevé'd while putting her tote bag in the overhead compartment, she was not a dancer. It was a gross act of cultural appropriation.

More than half the girls (and boys) were from Long Island and came on this trip with their friends. I'd signed up for the trip alone—and now questioned that decision. A huddle of girls fixed their mascara and eyeshadow as they balanced hand mirrors between their fingers or organized the contents of their Gucci purses. I was in foreign (enemy?) territory. The kids in my school shopped at Talbots and L.L.Bean. They definitely weren't trendy teenage fashionistas like these chicks were. I wore my standard uniform of jeans and a T-shirt. I wondered if I'd misread the tour description. Were we going to be pitching tents and hiking in Bryce Canyon in the summer heat or going to a fancy dinner party?

Yes, I judged the books by their covers. Because the covers were unfamiliar and I feared that I had nothing in common with them. I'd be sitting alone, eating corn dogs while watching cowboys and clowns at the Cody Rodeo in Wyoming.

When we piled into the motorcoach in Denver, I panicked. Where to sit, and with whom? It's always a nerve-wracking experience. I glommed onto a few girls who invited me to join them up front, behind Rodney, our bus driver. Rodney was probably forty and dipped chewing tobacco. He always had a pinch between his cheek and gum. His driving was also sometimes erratic. I was sure that he was catnapping behind the wheel on a few occasions. The girls were friendly, and they'd also come on the trip alone. They weren't cool by high school standards, and their clothing choices were understated but confident. They weren't out to impress, and I admired that. Still, we weren't cut from the same cloth—they lacked a certain pizzazz, which made it difficult for me to connect or find any common ground—other than being on the same bus.

My braces had come off the year before, and I'd recently ditched glasses for contact lenses. After several years of bad haircuts, my hair was flourishing—it'd come into its own and was having a moment. For the first time, I felt attractive—which is not ever how I described myself. The tour was an opportunity for me and my bouncy hair, straight teeth, and unobstructed green eyes to experience the flip side of theater nerd and average athlete.

There's no easy way to jump friend groups without stepping on a few toes when teenage girls are involved. But after two days, I found another group who were more my speed and who better suited my style. They were at the back of the bus—where everyone knows the popular kids sit. And now I was sitting with them. The view was pretty great. It wasn't anything like high school.

Most of the conversations with my new friends centered around sex. It was all vague and, at the same time, boastful—and all of it intriguing. I didn't have a lot of experience talking to male peers about anything related to sex. It was rarely discussed, even with my girlfriends at home. Between play rehearsals and basketball practice, it wasn't a priority. That's what summers were for.

I was a fly on the wall and kept quiet, waiting to see what I was up against before weighing in. What level of experience was I dealing with, and how much lying would be required? There was a lot of flirting and posturing. Some of the guys described situations that sounded like scenes right out of the television show *The Thorn Birds*. They passed them off as their own. But what they didn't know was that, as a TV addict, I knew they were full of shit.

The real juicy truth-telling happened at night when we girls were alone in the tent. They'd list sexual positions and experiences that they hadn't done, wouldn't do, and didn't know how to—but would like to do. It was a complete surprise to learn that I was the most experienced teen in the tent.

The previous summer, I'd gone to a theater camp. It was my debut both as a lead actress and as an object of sexual desire. Gary was seventeen, muscular, and smelled like a combination of Irish

Spring soap and roast beef (he worked in the camp kitchen). My roommates and I snuck out of our room almost nightly, climbing down fire escapes and hiding in bathrooms to get to the techie wing, where Gary and the kitchen staff slept. These guys were men—rugged, rough, and heterosexual. It was dangerous and heart-pumping. Gary would've been fired if we'd gotten caught, and my first starring role playing Roxie Hart in the musical *Chicago* would've been stripped away.

The first time Gary and I kissed was during a Fourth of July fireworks celebration. I was aroused, and I wanted more. I remember thinking, *Why are we still dressed?* The word "horny" was floating around high school that year, though no one dared take a stab at defining it or giving an in-depth explanation. I wondered if that's what I was feeling. The throbbing and fluttering throughout my body were so intense that I thought we'd orgasmed. Together. Simultaneously. At ages fourteen and seventeen. "Orgasm" was another word that was floating around unexplained.

Gary and I had only gone to second base, but it felt so much further—and still further than my tentmates.

And then I met Brian, one of the cool boys, at the back of the bus. He was seventeen, sexy, a track star with a lean body and mop of wavy dark hair. I got butterflies just looking at him. It was an immediate infatuation. But he was mysterious and hard to read. I couldn't tell if he was stuck up or just shy. I hadn't dared to try talking to him because, although my hair felt all that, the rest of me had a way to go.

We went climbing at the Crow Peak Trail in Badlands National Park, South Dakota, one afternoon. I felt like Grizzly Adams with my canteen slung over my shoulder and a bag of trail mix in my backpack. And then it happened. Brian and I made eye contact. He'd noticed me. We talked and laughed for hours until we reached the summit, where we stopped and ate lunch with the rest of the group. It was easy and casual with him, like we'd always been together.

Brian and I were quickly inseparable and became an item somewhere between the light show at Mount Rushmore and the eruption of Old Faithful in Yellowstone National Park. The hottest and funniest guy on the tour wanted to be with me. It was a beautiful miracle. He wasn't afraid to be silly, often strutting around in his running shorts and hiking boots like a model on the catwalk. He was also from Long Island, and I thought he was exotic because his parents were divorced. I didn't know anyone whose parents were divorced.

As much as I looked forward to staying together for the duration of the summer, I didn't let myself think about what would happen when it was over. After all, Brian was a senior. I'd been down this road before.

The teen tour brochure promised sightseeing, thrilling adventures, and lasting friendships. But it was more like adolescent hormone-fueled explorations. While the group discovered the Black Hills and the inmate gardens at Alcatraz, Brian and I discovered each other's bodies. And we were both wonderlands. I remember doing laundry at a Laundromat in Lake Tahoe. Brian had run out of underwear, so he went commando. I didn't know until he pushed me away when I went in for a hug. "Don't come near me." I smiled awkwardly. I didn't entirely understand the relationship between hanging loose and unconfined and what getting aroused might look like in one's paper-thin shorts.

My sex education came from Judy Blume books, like *Forever* (which I forgot to return to Olivia Dominguez). It's about two teenagers, Katherine and Michael's, first time. It was also the first time I saw the word "penis" in print. After I read it in fifth grade, I brought it to school. I had underlined the dirty parts, or what I thought were the dirty parts, and read them out loud on the blacktop at recess. "Then he was on top of me, and I felt Ralph, hard, against my thigh." Michael named his penis Ralph, and from then on, whenever I hear the name Ralph, I think "cock." Ralph Lauren, Cock Lauren. Cock Macchio. Cock Waldo Emerson.

My little show-and-tell got me in big trouble with the school nurse, Ms. Fogarty. She called my mom and me into her office and told us that the book was inappropriate for my age. *Inappropriate? I thought. My dad wears Speedos to the public pool, and my parents roll joints in the car before PTA meetings.* Ms. Fogarty waited for my mom to respond. Mom looked up from her wristwatch. "I'm just glad she can read."

On a sunny afternoon on Rodeo Drive in Beverly Hills, my romantic relationship with Brian came dangerously close to going up in flames. Out of nowhere, another teen tour was in town. The boys in our group, including Brian, started flirting and getting pretty chummy with the new girls. Every time we ran into them, the boys acted as if they'd never seen tits before. They completely ignored us. It was hurtful. It was also the first time I'd experienced jealousy in this way. Sure, I was jealous of any actress starring in *Annie*, but this new kind of jealousy was strange and ugly. I thought Brian and I had developed a deep connection and genuinely liked each other. Why would he treat me like this?

I'm ashamed to admit it, but I'd convinced myself that Brian's wandering blue eyes were because we hadn't gone all the way. And then Jeff, Brian's closest friend on the tour, validated my suspicions.

"Brian doesn't think you're interested in sex."

"What?" I was shocked and defensive. "Why would he think that?" Jeff shrugged.

I opened my journal later that night. "Dear Fiorucci, it's not true. It isn't. They don't know me. No one knows me. I wanted to tell Jeff all sorts of stuff, but I couldn't think fast enough."

At fifteen, I had no idea how to express intimate feelings about boys, being in love, and doing it—other than with poetry, that is. I had one more poem in me.

How could this happen?
Is it happening too fast?
When did it happen?
Will this happening last?

Brian and I hadn't discussed sleeping together—in the biblical sense. We were definitely pleasuring each other, so why would he think I'd want to stop there? He had no idea how interested and horny I was. When I got home from camp the summer before, I'd looked up "horny" in my *Encyclopedia Britannica*. But the only definition I found was of a horny sponge, which is a sea sponge. And I knew that wasn't right. I couldn't ask my friends because after my public reading of *Forever*, they considered me a kind of prepubescent Dr. Ruth. I didn't want to disappoint them with the truth—that the only naked body I'd seen up to that point was the red-headed girl holding an airplane on the cover of my parents' *Blind Faith* album.

I found an erotic book on my parents' bookshelf—ew—and read a rudimentary explanation.

If having sex would solidify my relationship with Brian, then so be it. I refused to let the rival teen skanks tempt my boyfriend. I was motivated and eager to lose my virginity. I never saw it as a big deal to begin with. Or necessarily something to save for a rainy day. I'd be the first one of my friends back home, paving the way for those coming up behind me. I could impart sage and wise advice when it was over. Friends would salute my maturity and my command of all things sex!

On the bus the next day, Brian and I settled into what had become *our* seat. I started to rub his thigh near his balls. He got an erection almost instantly. I giggled silently. *Oh, I get it.*

Brian moaned quietly.

"What's the matter?" I whispered. It sounded like I was hurting him.

"Nothing. It just feels good."

The next time we saw that other tour, Brian pulled me to him and held me tight. He apologized for being a douche and for disrespecting me. He assured me it was a misunderstanding and wouldn't happen again.

We drove through the iconic Paramount Studios gate to see the taping of the pilot for *Cheers*. It was my first time on a television sound stage. Brian and I sat beside each other in the first row, just above the stage, but close enough to see Ted Danson's pores.

After just ten minutes of taping, however, I was bored. There were too many stops and starts. And I also didn't like the show. I turned to Brian. "This is so bad. It'll never make it."

The sexual discoveries continued for the remainder of the trip.

The hand jobs performed over clothes graduated to bare skin under Brian's running shorts and tighty-whities. It was the first time I'd felt a naked penis. Hand jobs became blow jobs somewhere near Reno, Nevada.

One night, sleeping under the stars among the red rocks in Bryce Canyon, Brian turned to me in our shared sleeping bag. It was stupidly easy to sneak off by ourselves. Our so-called chaperones were too busy smoking dope and hooking up with each other to notice what we were up to.

"I want to make love to you," Brian cooed. I'm not sure those were his exact words. But he did tell me that he wanted to be my first.

I told him I wanted the same thing and added that I'd like to be in a cozy bed under a roof and not outside in a smelly campsite. The pebbles and thorny branches were poking me in the ribs.

By the end of the summer, I had a boyfriend, my own Ralph, and I'd made lasting friendships. Brian and I said goodbye at JFK airport, crying on each other's shoulders. We promised to call and to get together as soon as possible. Leaving him was painful. I started to tell him that I loved him, but I choked up. My words couldn't steer themselves around the lump in my throat. What I'd felt about Alan Reeves, né Adelson, was a schoolgirl crush—it was a show-mance. Brian and I were in love.

Two weeks before my sixteenth birthday in September, Brian and I went to a Clash concert in Manhattan. After the show, we took a train to his house on Long Island. I can't remember the lie I told my parents that allowed the sleepover. Brian and I agreed that it would be *the* night. The night that, according to everyone, would change my life and make me a woman. I was anxious to experience what everyone was talking about.

When we arrived at his house, where his mom was not, I crawled up the stairs to Brian's bedroom. I'd worn new leather boots, and they were crippling me. Still, I stayed laser-focused on the task at hand. The time and place couldn't have been more ideal. We weren't in the back seat of a car or on top of a pile of coats on some random friend's waterbed at a Halloween party.

Brian and I lay on his twin bed underneath his black polyester blanket for a few silent moments. All the while, I was trusting that he knew what to do. I mean, I thought it'd be self-explanatory, but there's always a chance for a curveball. And I hoped that I wouldn't look like a complete novice. Brian made his move while I stared at the glow-in-the-dark solar system on the ceiling. I wondered which bright dot above was the sun and which was Earth. I also thought about Katherine and Michael's first time and if what was happening on top of me would be the same. And just when I found the moon, Brian was lying beside me.

"Was that it?" I asked when it was over. I was genuinely curious. Brian smiled.

It was astonishingly anticlimactic—the train ride to Long Island had more twists and turns. And it was quick, the same way it happened in *Forever*. But whereas Katherine was disappointed, as she was not satisfied, I didn't care. It was satisfying enough, I guess. There was no way I knew what being satisfied meant anyway. What was most important and meaningful to me was that this supposed monumental event was with someone I loved and cared about.

I went into the bathroom to see if some transformation had taken place and was visible on my face. Perhaps a celebration was in full swing in my vagina. Much to my disappointment, there wasn't a mariachi band playing. And I didn't look any different from how I'd looked three and a half minutes earlier. It wasn't anything like in the movies or on TV.

While continuing my search for a hint of afterglow, I felt something squishy between my legs. *What the hell?* I screamed in a stage whisper. The tip of the condom was hanging out of my vagina—which meant that the rest of it was still inside of me. To be clear, I wasn't sure that that wasn't supposed to happen. I hadn't read about this kind of stuff in any of Judy's books. I did entertain the possibility that I was somehow responsible. Maybe I'd done something wrong. I don't remember studying this in sex education classes in school. We weren't taught how to apply condoms using cucumbers or zucchini. Nor how to remove them properly and safely.

Brian should've known what to do and taken care of it. I was the virgin, after all.

After I retrieved the half-shriveled rubber, I didn't know what to do with it. *Do I flush it? What if it backs up the toilet? Do I throw it out? What if his mom finds it?* I contemplated taking it home and pressing it in my Fiorucci notebook. But then I wondered if Brian would wonder where it'd gotten off to. If I'd been more self-possessed and honest about my knowledge (or lack thereof), I would've asked the boy half asleep in his twin bed, "What the hell just happened?"

But I wasn't any of those things. I was self-conscious and ill-equipped to ask for an explanation. Besides, Brian seemed too satisfied with himself. I didn't want to spoil the moment with such a silly thing like a wayward prophylactic.

So I left it on the side of the bathtub. It was Brian's problem now.

I was sure Brian would mention the incident the next time we spoke. He'd educate me on why this sometimes happens and assure me it wasn't my fault. I also wanted to know if I had to take a pregnancy test. From that incident going forward, it didn't matter what forms of protection my partners and I used, be it a spacesuit or beekeeping coveralls—I never entirely trusted.

Brian and I spoke the following day. His voice was soft and sheepish. "Yeah, I'm sorry about that. I don't know what happened."

"Wait, was that your first time too?"

"Uh-huh."

For some reason, he'd assumed that I knew. Thankfully, Brian and I left it at that—no follow-up questions or further probing necessary. Instead, we laughed like two embarrassed and naïve adolescents in love. And I begged time to stop because I knew that innocence like ours wouldn't last forever.

eleven

Baader-Meinhof Phenomenon?

WHY SHOULDN'T I CALL the actor Christopher Meloni my spiritual mentor? Fairy Godfather sounds silly.

I've been getting symbolic pushes and intangible warnings from Christopher for years. It's as if he points me in the right direction when I'm going through challenging times. Like when I'm indecisive, losing my bearings, or chasing my tail. When I'm in these states, he appears to me (in some form) to help me navigate them. That's my interpretation of these "events" anyway. His timing is impeccable. I've relied on his psychic gestures time and again. Christopher Meloni's helping hands are like having my own symphony conductor.

When I considered divorcing my husband in early 2001, I went back and forth, deliberating about the hows and whys and who keeps Little Ricky. In my gut, I wanted the divorce. But I didn't always trust my gut. I'd said "I do" six years earlier despite that bitch yelling, "No! You don't!" So I was still somewhat skeptical and scared to pull the trigger. I needed some indication that I was making the right decision. Then, on a Tuesday night in April, I turned on the television to take a break from my pros and cons list—which was now a two-volume set. Christopher was on screen in a movie trailer for *Wet Hot American Summer*, a raunchy comedy about the last day of summer in 1981. "I'm going to fondle my sweater," says Christopher's character, a camp kitchen staff member. Come on—camp, comedy, sweaters? Could Chris have been any more obvious? He was all the affirmation I needed. I was divorced three months later.

So, yeah, I pay attention and attach meaning to Christopher's signs and celestial messages—they're constant, reliable, and straightforward.

It began at the gym where he was a member and where I worked during my senior year at college. We were both struggling artists in the city, him as an actor and I as a filmmaker-producer-writer-performer. When Christopher stopped at the front desk, our eyes met.

"Towel?" I asked.

"Sure," he answered.

It was almost like a mating call. Although our relationship, which he knew nothing about, was never romantic.

In the early '90s, we both moved to Los Angeles. Things started to pick up for Christopher right away. He had a starring role on the television show *The Fanelli Boys* and was in the movie *Junior*. I auditioned for game show pilots and the lead broccoli stalk in a Beano commercial. It wasn't a competition, but as the captain of my career, I looked honestly at my situation, which didn't resemble Christopher's career at all.

Sometimes I spent weeks in bed, too sad and blue to brush my teeth or eat. I watched TV from sunup to sundown—before it was trendy binge-watching, it was called depression. One morning, I ran out of coffee filters. My cup of joe was the only thing I looked forward to in those days. So I pulled myself together, slid off my bed, and put on the yoga pants and sports bra lying in the pile on the floor.

Next to the grocery store was a gym called Trooper Fitness. It offered a boot camp class I'd wanted to try but hadn't gotten around to. If I couldn't find the strength to run a comb through my hair or pick up a Waterpik, there was no way I could swing a barbell or hurl myself over a wall. I peered into the window. Men and women were lined up in rows, touching their toes, circling their arms—warming up for the class that was about to start. And then something got my attention. Or should I say, someone got my attention. Standing by the monkey bars, adjusting her hair scrunchie, was the actress Stephanie March, a.k.a. Assistant District Attorney Alexandra Cabot from *Law & Order: SVU.*

Christopher had sent a surrogate.

And just like that, I found my motivation and walked inside. Luckily, there was an open spot, and I joined Stephanie and the others. She was my reward for getting dressed and leaving my apartment—a metaphorical thumbs up. Christopher knew what I needed, and there it was.

That's how things worked with Christopher.

His guidance floats on mystical waves that sometimes wash up on shore at my feet. When I hesitated to take an adult tap dance class, he appeared on an episode of *NYPD Blue* alongside my theater camp acting coach. I shuffle-ball-changed to class the following morning. And after a horrible breakup and sobbing uncontrollably in the Ralph's parking lot in Burbank, a bus drove by and on the side was a photo of a half-naked Christopher in an ad for *Oz*, the TV show he was then starring in. It was confirmation that breaking up with my narcissistic attorney boyfriend was the right decision and I was better off without him. With each perfectly timed appearance, Christopher gives me his seal of approval or admonishes me to stop what I'm doing and jump ship.

A few months after Christopher lifted me out from under my blahs, I walked away from my big Hollywood dreams. My ambition and stubbornness, which had helped push me forward over the years, stopped working. It'd all become harder to manufacture. I'd concussed myself too many times banging my head (and efforts) against the wall. That's when I sold my belongings, left California, and moved to Prague to teach English. And when that didn't work out, I made a phone call.

Tina and Randy, the married travel agents I'd met in Prague, put me in touch with their friend Theresa. She was a filmmaker who was organizing a video production class for disadvantaged girls in Granada, Nicaragua. I was so unmoored and aimless after Prague that it sounded like as good an idea as any. After a brief conversation with Theresa, she offered me a position documenting the girls as they learned about the magic of moviemaking.

"Oh," I said, "like VH1's *Behind the Music*?"

"Huh?"

Here I was, again being seduced by show business after I'd just walked away. Prague and the English language were definitely far afield, but documentary filmmaking was at least in my wheelhouse. I rationalized that the circumstances were very different. I was doing something meaningful and helpful. My volunteering and perhaps bettering myself was a sincere proposition. Granada was a chance to combine my creative and humanitarian sides—I could be selfless while trying to find myself. I paid for my transportation, food, and anything else that might keep me alive in the jungle. Dengue fever was spreading throughout Nicaragua, but I didn't care. Central America was a singular offer. I'd be a benevolent Ken Burns in the barrio.

However, this whole time, Christopher had been oddly silent. I didn't hear from him before I moved to Prague or accepted Theresa's proposition in Nicaragua. Dun-dun.

Theresa and I planned to meet at the Miami airport, fly to Managua, the capital of Nicaragua, and then drive to Granada. I landed in Miami; Theresa did not. Her plane was delayed in Michigan and she'd missed her connecting flight. And then I realized I'd be flying to Managua alone. Wandering around at night, alone, as a woman who doesn't speak Spanish seemed like a bad idea and an *SVU* episode. The room started spinning. Where was Christopher? His signals had never taken this long.

I lumbered to the Avianca Airlines gate in a panic—my heart racing, my armpits wet. I told myself over and over that I could bail and turn around. Nobody would care. And then I thought about my duffel bag—it was checked through to Managua. What would happen to it if I wasn't there to pick it up? I'd sold sixteen years' worth of possessions when I moved to Prague, but suddenly, I couldn't live without my rain pants and a headlamp.

A flight attendant showed me to my seat, and I forced a smile. There was still time to make a run for it. But what about the kids? The barrio was depending on me. I gripped the armrests and tapped my toes nervously. I silently promised whomever (or whatever) was in control of the plane that if we didn't crash, I'd stop judging people who carry small snaggle-toothed dogs in BabyBjörns.

"Is this your first trip to Nicaragua?" my seatmate asked once we were airborne. I hadn't noticed her until that moment. I'm not religious, but when I saw this zaftig woman's enormous wooden cross necklace, I thought, *Definitely the person I want sitting next to me if we fall out of the sky.*

Sylvia was a nurse with sturdy shoulders and bright, purplish hair. She was bringing medical supplies to villages and churches throughout Nicaragua. I projectile vomited words and worry into her face. "How far is Granada from Managua? How am I going to get there? Is there a bus? Train? Should I stay somewhere tonight? Can you hear my heart pounding?"

She looked into my watery eyes. "I'm happy to take you to the hotel where I'm staying." She was all compassion. "It's close to the airport. We'll get you to Granada in the morning." I nodded with a vacant stare and thanked her.

The last available room at the Best Western was meat-locker cold. The air conditioner coughed and sputtered. I didn't dare turn it off because it was ninety-four degrees outside and a hundred percent humidity inside. I dropped into a squat on the floor in front of the two twin beds and stared at the peeling popcorn ceiling. I was inhaling asbestos for sure. My lungs would be scarred by morning.

My skin itched, and I pulled at the fine hairs on my arms. My agitation ramped up. *Should I stay? Should I go? Stay—finish what you started. Leave—this isn't right.* The questions were relentless and paralyzing. I was caught in a game of tug-of-war. *What do I want? Why don't I know?*

When I left Los Angeles for Prague, I'd severed the umbilical cord between myself and show business. But it wasn't until I sat on the stained motel room carpet that I felt like I just might float away. Standing in front of the cracked porcelain sink, I scarfed down my last (and now melted) protein bar. I turned on the small television and unconsciously flipped through the channels. A few seconds of a soap opera, a football game, and then a talk show. I grabbed the pack of cigarettes on the side table. I thought smoking would distract and calm me. It didn't. And now I smelled like burnt motor oil.

A cockroach the size of a newborn's foot scurried out from underneath the bed. I felt powerless to kill it, and instead, I lit the last cigarette.

"Stuff came up," I emailed Theresa. "I may not be able to join you." I didn't know what else to say. I was afraid to tell her that I was having a change of heart because I didn't want to appear wishy-washy and confused. Theresa was too noble for that. My explanation sounded cagey, like I was in witness protection, not a woman reassessing a plan.

This fearful and strung-out person wasn't me.

Just as I was about to turn off the television, there he was, on Channel 6—Christopher on *SVU*. He was running pigeon-toed in tight synthetic pants that outlined his firm and arresting ass. He chased a perp down a crowded street in Harlem while growling for backup in perfect undubbed English. His request for backup was code for "leave Nicaragua." Forcing back tears, I yelled, "What took you so long?"

I tossed my toiletries back into my suitcase.

Adios.

Twelve hours after landing, I was back at the Managua airport.
A friend from LA was traveling around the Netherlands, and I
thought that if I saw a familiar face and took some time to regroup,
I'd feel a whole lot better.

"I'd like to get on the first available flight to Amsterdam," I told
the KLM agent. I handed her my return ticket to JFK, hoping she
could change the destination city.

She put down her book and yawned. "Are you sure? You just
got in last night."

Was it illegal to visit Nicaragua for less than twenty-four hours?
I did look disheveled, and I reeked. I might've looked suspicious,
too. *Does she think I'm a drug mule?* My stomach cramped, imagining the cocaine-filled balloons in my intestines. A paragraph on the
National Library of Medicine's website says the most commonly
used body parts for smuggling are the entire gastrointestinal tract,
"from mouth to anus." I do not know why or when I looked this up.

I'd be a terrible smuggler. When it came time to force-feed me
laxatives so I could shit out the illicit drugs, I wouldn't be able to,
especially if the laxatives were the over-the-counter kind. Years ago,
preparing for a colonoscopy, I'd drunk the standard bowel prep, but
when I was on the exam table, my doctor couldn't thoroughly probe
me because I was still full of shit—I guess I don't like to let things
go. She had to prescribe a horse-strength concoction. Only then did
I crap a crystal-clear river. I'm too high maintenance for someone
like El Chapo. He wouldn't put up with my fussy needs.

For the next several weeks, I hopped around Europe, from Anne
Frank's attic to Auschwitz. I waited for another sign from Christopher. After visiting the Holmenkollen Ski Museum, where I saw
a pair of thousand-year-old skis (snooze), I got very lost in the

woods looking for the Holmenkollen-Kapelle-Sprungschanze-Holmenkollen loop hiking trail. When I reemerged two hours later, I returned to my hotel room in Oslo and checked my email. And there he was.

My friend Andy told me Christopher was starring in the play *A View from the Bridge* at the Gate Theater in Dublin. Andy knew all about Christopher and me, adding, "You have to go. You're so close."

"Who cares about my fear of flying? What's another two and a half hours?" I screamed to no one in the shower of my hotel bathroom. My fear of flight hasn't kept me from the friendly skies, only because I've discovered magical little yellow pills.

Going to Dublin felt natural; it was a chance to see my spiritual mentor face-to-face after so many years. I was excited. It felt like I was going to support a close friend. Christopher would welcome me with open arms, a fellow countryman (countryperson?) from his homeland to hang out with—he was probably lonely. Did anyone in Ireland even know who Christopher Meloni was? There wasn't any way he'd draw the kind of crowd in Dublin that he did in New York or LA. Reaching out and inviting him to meet me for a drink after the show seemed reasonable. I pictured our reunion over a chilled lager and a bowl of Irish stew.

Imagine my surprise when the box office attendant at the theater told me the show had sold out. I guess he was popular in Ireland after all. The cheery woman in the box office told me to return at seven o'clock in case tickets became available because of last-minute cancellations. Seeing Christopher now hinged on someone getting into a car accident or going into labor.

I moved away from the box office and tore out a blank sheet from my journal. "Dear Christopher . . ." I invited him out after the show and thanked him for rescuing me in Nicaragua. And I told him how much his subtle guidance had meant to me over the years. I also wanted him to know we had a history beyond the gym, so I listed the people we had in common—it was all very six degrees of Kevin Bacon. It was more than eight connections and included his friend who'd died on September 11 who was also an acquaintance of a friend of mine. It was a risky move, but I wasn't thinking straight. When I reread the note, I thought it sounded quite endearing.

"Would you please give this to Mr. Meloni?" I asked the woman at the box office. I slid the note through the slot under the plexiglass. She took the folded paper, stared at it as if she'd misheard me, and then looked up. I met her gaze with self-assurance. For all she knew, I was Christopher's business manager and the note was a past-due invoice.

I started down the front steps of the theater—feeling proud for taking the initiative, even though I was a little intimidated. And then I saw my sneakers. The grime and rips, visual evidence of my travels, made it look like I'd walked the entire island of Ireland, sweeping up after livestock. Christopher deserved better. A friendly young man directed me to a department store near the theater.

Luckily, the first shoes I tried on were also the last. I hate shopping. They were bile-colored, block-heeled ankle boots made of plastic or rubber—it was hard to tell. I took a few steps on the linoleum floor. They were slightly uncomfortable, but it didn't matter. I was on the clock. And where was I going, in and out of the theater? To a local pub? They were more like visual props.

At six o'clock sharp, I was back at the Gate Theater. I sat on the front steps and waited for the line for rush tickets to open. I untied my sneakers and pulled up my white athletic socks. I should've bought a pair of dress socks. And why boots? It was August. I crossed my right foot over my left knee for leverage. It took a bit of force to wedge my foot into my boot. Several droplets from my forehead and cheeks fell onto my sleeve. I wiped my face. And then, in the distance, I saw a figure.

It was Christopher Meloni.

Traffic came to a standstill, and someone turned on a fog machine. Christopher sailed through the clouds of smoke, almost walking on air, emerging in three-dimensional technicolor.

I stared at him fifty feet away. A brown leather backpack was flung over his broad shoulders, and he was clutching a script to his barrel chest. It was positively bizarre. And then, I could've sworn there was a moment of recognition on his face: "*I know you.*"

I panicked. What now? My shoe was dangling from my foot, and sweat was dripping down my flushed face.

It was one thing to experience Christopher's ethereal presence—I could mold it to suit my needs. Use it to make me feel like I wasn't losing my shit. Assure me that my creative pursuits weren't in vain. His love taps (illusory or not) worked for me. But Christopher in the flesh?

He started up the steps, as if in slow motion, toward the entrance to the theater.

I'd come this far—I had to carpe diem. It's too bad I couldn't ask Christopher what he thought I should do. I took a deep breath and started to stand. As I did, my right heel caught the cuff of my left pant leg, and I nearly face-planted onto the concrete. I felt Christopher's piercing blue eyes sear into the back of my head as I teetered on one leg, trying to right myself. I looked like a clumsy, theater-loving oaf who was also probably drunk. I lowered my head, looked away, and silently begged him to keep walking—and not try to help me.

Christopher disappeared as quickly as he'd appeared, and I kicked myself with my bile-colored boot for the missed opportunity.

After waiting in line for nearly an hour, I got a ticket. I hobbled to my seat in the very last row of the balcony. I barely remember Christopher's performance or the show because while his character, Eddie Carbone, was wrestling with his passionate fury for his niece, I was plotting.

I'll wait by the stage door during the curtain call. If Christopher gets my note, he'll be expecting me. But what if he gets my note and sneaks out the back door? What if he doesn't get my note, but I see him at the stage door? Should I act out the message?

Crowds of people holding theater programs with their cameras poised huddled around the stage door. I got nervous and moved away from the crowd. Instead, I pretended to talk to someone on my cell phone. An urgent business matter had come up, and I was putting out a fire and not loitering like a fan. I wasn't a fan. I knew Christopher Meloni.

Setting myself up for the possibility of another awkward situation didn't deter me. I'd written the note, and in a perfect world, Miss Box Office Lady had delivered it per my instructions. I had to follow through. After a long and overdue embrace, I'd apologize to Christopher for not saying hello to him on the front steps. Then again, maybe he hadn't even noticed me, my boots, or my clumsiness. And if that were the case, I wouldn't have to address it at all.

After twenty minutes, the crowd dispersed. Christopher hadn't come out to greet his fans—or maybe I'd missed him because I was on the phone. I lingered for a while longer, until I was the only one left, and then turned away from the theater.

I started back toward my hotel, limping along Granby Road. I paused every few steps to look over my shoulder—just in case. What if Christopher was waiting for me in front of the theater? What if he did get my note and I'd left too soon? After all, he had to remove his stage makeup and change out of his costume into his street clothes. I turned around and headed back toward the theater—I had to be sure. I didn't want to kick myself a second time for missing him.

With all my lingering and pacing back and forth, up and down the streets in my ridiculous boots, I looked like a working girl.

The theater was still off in the distance, but the streets were empty and dark. It was over.

At any other time, I might've laughed at my behavior, but so much had happened over the past several months, so much transition, searching, and chaos, that all I felt was dejected and embarrassed.

I turned around again and walked away.

When I reached my hotel, I changed into my pajamas and climbed into bed. Well, that didn't turn out at all the way I'd planned. I'd gone too far. Why couldn't I be satisfied with the divine interventions and leave it at that? I felt like an ass. I was still living in some fantasy world—which hadn't been a problem up until then. But it wasn't gratifying anymore; nor was it doing me any good. Taking inventory of my life and seeing where I was headed wasn't a terrible idea. It's just that it hadn't occurred to me until I walked the streets of Dublin.

A few months later, I was sprawled out on my couch in my new apartment in Hell's Kitchen. I'd moved to New York without knowing what I would do once I got there. But I was also confident that

I'd figure it out. I was watching episode two of season eight of *SVU*. The episode introduced a new character, a Danish detective sent in to replace Detective Olivia Benson while she was on an undercover assignment. The new girl's name was Dani Beck. I bolted up. Christopher had received my note after all! He'd been with me all along. Detective Beck's appearance meant that Christopher validated my move to New York and applauded me for trusting myself and taking the leap.

"Towel?"

Poetry in (E)Motion

Unexpected Relationship

It all seemed so simple, the way I quickly fell,
For it happens so very often, but of which I cannot tell.
The warnings and the lectures, the sermons, and the pleadings,
I'm just a girl who sees for herself and knows that she is needing.
I try to tell myself that seriousness may be deadly,
But how can I help my true feelings which flow out like a melody?
Our talk was more than words released,
Our ideas and emotions said what we felt and who we are.
To say to someone, "I love you," is sharing a very personal part of
     yourself,
It has to take someone very special in order for it to hold true.
There's an attraction that I feel between us, although I don't
     know why,
It's hard to get romantically close to you, the frustration I feel inside.
You're on my mind probably more than you should be,

And so, I've turned a simple hello into something that I have
    to control.
Not you but me!

Now He's Gone!

Can anyone know what I'm going through,
Relaxing here thinking of you?
Depression sinks in when I recall,
How long you'll be gone.
I try not to think of that but it seems much too long.
It may seem selfish, but I don't care,
Oh, my love, I wish I were there.
Who would have guessed who would have thought
that a simple acquaintance, love could be brought?

Thinking About . . .

How could this happen?
Is it happening too fast?
When did it happen?
Will this happening last?

Pondering

Do I want it to be public?
Why am I afraid?
Is this happening too fast?
Can I handle the situation?

Are my feelings changing?
Why aren't I thinking about him more?
Please tell me what's in store.

Realizing

I love when you call,
but really that's not all.
As you said with the other
It was getting a bore.
So, if you don't call so often,
When you do, I'll love it even more.

Shitting Around

Right now I'm in math,
But I could imagine a warm bath.
Today we got our yearbooks,
We all had our looks,
But I was pinned on your photograph.
Yes, I'm sitting here in math.

Growing Impatient

To wait on one just to make sure of the other, holds me back to sit
    and think.
Would everything fall into place with a blink?
I want to believe, to need and love. Why is it, though, that I get
    the attached ones.

Foolish thoughts, I do want something special.

Now I have to be strong, that is the essential.

Hurry home before I don't care, why I haven't a clue.

But always remember that I do love you.

Doubting

The time blew away as if nothing could have stopped it.

Knowing what's ahead now makes it difficult to open the eyes.

You want to trust and feel you'll always be told the truth.

Caution steps in and to avoid getting hurt you take the safe path.

Acknowledgments

A HEARTFELT THANK-YOU to my early readers, editors, and friends, who listened patiently to my complaining and monkey brain: Emily, Coley, Leslie, Muffy, Wendy, Alison (Lady), Naomi, Aimee, Beth, Robin A, and Auntie I. And to my parents and brother for the steady stream of material.

Forgive me if I've forgotten anyone.

About the Author

Photo by Seth Pomerantz

DANI ALPERT is the author of the memoir *The Girlfriend Mom*, winner of the 2020 Story Circle Network Gilda Award for comedy, honoring Gilda Radner. She spent decades working in theater, television, and film, performing, writing, and directing. She is a Pilates instructress and an advocate for the Down syndrome community. Dani's first headshot was her mugshot, taken after she was arrested for tagging when she was a juvenile. She's been trying to reclaim those glory days ever since.